ARE YOU
READY?

UNDERSTANDING
GOD'S FINAL CHAPTER

Nate Grahl

ISBN 978-1-64471-661-8 (Paperback)
ISBN 978-1-64471-662-5 (Hardcover)
ISBN 978-1-64471-663-2 (Digital)

Covenant Books, Inc.
11661 Hwy 707
Murrells Inlet, SC 29576
www.covenantbooks.com

Faith

believing without seeing

Calligraphy Designed By
Maria Grahl
www.wwapbglobal.com
@writewithapurpose

PREFACE

Revelation is meant to be understood. God had the Apostle John on the Isle of Patmos write it just like God spoke the parables through Jesus and the many stories of the Old Testament.

God used multiple stories to explain one aspect of Himself to help us understand Him even in our human state. Jesus told multiple parables explaining Heaven to mere humans. This task is impossible without the help of the Holy Spirit living and teaching us from within.

This book includes the full Holy Scripture from the King James Bible. I am not against any translation, but I believe, because of the Old English of the King James Bible, the Holy Spirit can show you even more as He illuminates the Scriptures to you.

When you finish this book, you will have read the whole book of Revelation and many other verses of the Bible. Many verses in this book are great verses to memorize. Please make the effort to memorize and hide God's Word in your heart. The Word of God will bless you in times of need more than you can imagine.

The first chapter of this book is meant to bring you into fellowship with your Creator God, Son of God, Jesus Christ, and the Holy Spirit. More will be explained within these pages, but please consider following the advice of chapter one before venturing on into the following chapters.

I stress the need to press into God, because if you do, you will multiply the joy of the following chapters by a hundredfold and beyond. Your understanding will be amazing by the work of God's Holy Spirit working supernaturally within you.

Don't worry. Pressing into God is simple and free. Please read on.

And have F-A-I-T-H! Yes, faith is the only way you can please God. Faith is *when you believe even though you have questions or do not have all the answers*. Some people demand to find all the answers and never choose to believe. Please do not be one of them.

Sooner or later, you must come to God and accept His free gift of salvation by faith in what Jesus Christ "did" (shed His sinless blood) on the cross of Calvary. Yes, only by believing without knowing all the answers. Please decide to just accept God's *free gift* today. God will give you answers in His time. Just believe!

1) Why did God speak to us in parables?
2) Who will illuminate the Scriptures for you if you allow Him?
3) Why don't you need to know all the answers before believing in what God did for you through Jesus?

Memory Verse: Hebrews 11:1

Freedom
Begins when you
Accept
God's
Existence

Calligraphy Designed By
Maria Grahl
www.wwapbglobal.com
@writewithapurpose

CHAPTER 1
ARE YOU READY FOR THE END?

Pre-Adam

Almighty God created the heavens and the earth.

> In the beginning God created the heaven and the
> earth (Genesis 1:1).

The Bible says that the "earth was without form and void" in verse two of Genesis one. God does not mention heaven in verse two. I believe that this is to mean that the earth was without life since it was also covered with water. I do not believe the earth was originally created covered with water.

When God cleansed the earth in the time of Noah with the flood, God confirmed that He would never destroy all flesh with a flood of water as written in Genesis 9:15. By this confession, I believe life was destroyed before Genesis 1:2 with a flood of water since verse two says, "the Spirit of God moved upon the waters."

I believe that God was developing the earth *just for us* for many more years than the six thousand years that was recorded in the Bible. We are told about some prehistoric events like the casting down of satan from heaven.

The verses below tell about satan (great red dragon), heaven's most beautiful angel, being cast out of heaven with a third of the angels, demons (third part of the stars of heaven). The "seven heads and ten horns" relate to Daniel's Prophecy.

> And there appeared another wonder in heaven;
> and behold a great red dragon, having seven
> heads and ten horns, and seven crowns upon his
> heads. 4 And his tail drew the third part of the
> stars of heaven, and did cast them to the earth:
> (Revelation 12:3–4)

I do believe that God created the earth *as we know it* in a six-day period. Frankly, God can do anything, so why should we doubt. Remember, our entire existence is based on F-A-I-T-H. Think about it!

You have faith in the driver next to you when you drive down the road, faith that a chair will hold you, faith that the air you breathe will keep you alive. I could fill this book with examples, but I believe you understand my point.

God gives us so many reasons to believe in His existence by creation alone. Freedom begins with your acceptance of God's existence. You can sense God's unconditional love for us in the beauty of His creations made *just for us*!

> And the earth was without form, and void; and
> darkness was upon the face of the deep. And the
> Spirit of God moved upon the face of the waters.
> (Genesis 1:2)

About 4,000 BC

Adam and Eve sinned.

> But of the fruit of the tree which is in the midst
> of the garden, God hath said, Ye shall not eat of
> it, neither shall ye touch it, lest ye die. ⁶And when
> the woman saw that the tree was good for food,
> and that it was pleasant to the eyes, and a tree to
> be desired to make one wise, she took of the fruit
> thereof, and did eat, and gave also unto her husband with her; and he did eat. (Genesis 3:3, 6)

Sin entered into God's perfect creation allowing satan to work through man to try and destroy what God lovingly meant for awesomeness. But God already had a plan for His creation, you and me.

> And the LORD God said unto the serpent, Because thou hast done this, thou art cursed above all cattle, and above every beast of the field; upon thy belly shalt thou go, and dust shalt thou eat all the days of thy life: [15]And I will put enmity between thee and the woman, and between thy seed and her seed; it shall bruise thy head, and thou shalt bruise his heel. (Genesis 3:14–15)

This Enmity, God was talking about, was going to be Himself in the body of Jesus Christ. God's plan was to allow satan to bruise Him, but God would be able to deliver the fatal blow to satan's head as a result of the bruise (death and resurrection). We now have the privilege of looking back at the plan and understand what God has done *just for us* at the cross of Calvary.

Until then, God gave Adam and Eve a plan to deal with their sin. They could not continue to experience the perfection of the Garden of Eden, but God wanted them to experience His presence. God instructed them that an innocent animal without blemish must be sacrificed annually as payment for their sins. Remember, a human had original sin passed on from Adam and could not be a sacrifice. This is evident by the story of Cain and Abel, sons of Adam and Eve.

> And in process of time it came to pass, that Cain brought of the fruit of the ground an offering unto the LORD. [4]And Abel, he also brought of the firstlings of his flock and of the fat thereof. And the LORD had respect unto Abel and to his offering: [5]But unto Cain and to his offering he had not respect. And Cain was very wroth, and his countenance fell. (Genesis 4:3-5)

You may read further, and you know that Cain killed Abel because Cain was so angry at God for not accepting his sacrifice for sin. I believe Cain went to his brother Abel to trade for a lamb many times before the time mentioned in Genesis chapter four. Abel was the keeper of the sheep, and his parents Adam and Eve probably came to him to trade as well.

About 2,000 BC

Before God could accomplish His ultimate plan for paying for our sin, He had to bring into being His holy people, Israel! As we look back in history, we must marvel at God's perseverance of the Israeli people. That alone is proof that God exists!

An innocent blood sacrifice was taught throughout the ages. Moses wrote down God's history and laws in the first five books of the Bible. We find the innocent blood sacrifice during the tenth plague on Egypt that freed the Jewish people from captivity. Innocent blood was applied to the door posts of each home that wanted the death angel to pass over them and not kill their firstborn son.

I believe that God may have been using satan himself as the "death angel." That night is remembered to this day as the Passover and is celebrated every year throughout the world by the Jewish people.

About 1,500 BC

And they shall take of the blood, and strike it on the two side posts and on the upper door post of the houses, wherein they shall eat it. [13]And the blood shall be to you for a token upon the houses where ye are: and when I see the blood, I will pass over you, and the plague shall not be upon you to destroy you, when I smite the land of Egypt. (Exodus 12:7, 13)

The Jewish people worshipped God, sinned by worshipping other gods, fell into captivity, and repented, turning back to their true God many times throughout the Old Testament. Many prophets of God spoke hundreds of prophecies concerning God's Savior for the human race. These prophecies were recorded so we would know, without any doubt, that Jesus is our Savior, the Lamb of God.

4 BC

Jesus fulfilled the prophecy that the Messiah or Savior would be born of a virgin in the small town of Bethlehem. The following scripture also proclaims that Jesus is our everlasting God. Amazing!

Jesus had to be born of a virgin, so the sin-nature would not pass onto Him. The fact that Jesus was not born of man's seed made Jesus the only person eligible to be our innocent sacrifice once and for all.

> Therefore the Lord himself shall give you a sign;
> Behold, a virgin shall conceive, and bear a son,
> and shall call his name Immanuel (God with us).
> (Isaiah 7:4)
>
> Wherefore, as by one man sin entered into the
> world, and death by sin; and so death passed upon
> all men, for that all have sinned: (Romans 5:12)

The following verses take us to the time of God coming to earth in the form of a baby by the name of Jesus. The woman is the Jewish people, and the twelve stars are the twelve tribes of Israel. The child delivered is our Savior and God, Jesus Christ.

The dragon is satan working through King Herod. The Three Kings of the east arrived in Jerusalem about two years after they saw the bright star in their eastern sky. The three foreign kings stopped by Herod. The religious leaders knew that God's Savior would be born in a small town of Bethlehem.

The Three Kings decided to travel to the small town of Bethlehem. King Herod wanted the Three Kings to let him know where Jesus was, so he could worship him as well. The kings were warned by God in a dream not to go back to Jerusalem, and they left for their country a different way.

King Herod found out that the kings left without informing
him, and he had all of the male children of Bethlehem, two years
old and younger, killed trying to destroy Jesus. God had already
informed Joseph, the earthly stepfather of Jesus, to take Mary and
Jesus to Egypt the night before the massacre, and Jesus was safe.

This event, in my opinion, lines up with John's vision in
Revelation chapter 12. It is interesting how God had the situation
covered. God had the Three Kings with precious gifts arrive just in
time to fund the unexpected journey and stay in Egypt while saving
Jesus. This event also fulfilled an unlikely prophecy that the Messiah
would come out of Egypt.

> But thou, Bethlehem Ephratah, though thou be
> little among the thousands of Judah, yet out of
> thee shall he come forth unto me that is to be
> ruler in Israel; whose goings forth have been from
> of old, from everlasting. (Micah 5:2)
>
> And there appeared a great wonder in
> heaven; a woman clothed with the sun, and the
> moon under her feet, and upon her head a crown
> of twelve stars: ²And she being with child cried,
> travailing in birth, and pained to be delivered.
> ⁴ᴮAnd the dragon stood before the woman which
> was ready to be delivered, for to devour her child
> as soon as it was born. (Revelation 12:1–2, 4b)
>
> And being warned of God in a dream that
> they should not return to Herod, they departed
> into their own country another way. ¹³And when
> they were departed, behold, the angel of the Lord
> appeareth to Joseph in a dream, saying, Arise, and
> take the young child and his mother, and flee into
> Egypt, and be thou there until I bring thee word:
> for Herod will seek the young child to destroy
> him. ¹⁴When he arose, he took the young child
> and his mother by night, and departed into Egypt:
> ¹⁵And was there until the death of Herod: that it

might be fulfilled which was spoken of the Lord by the prophet, saying, Out of Egypt have I called my son. (Matthew 2:12–15)

AD 27

As proclaimed by John the Baptist, Jesus was announced as the "Son of God" by God Himself. The account of John the Baptist and Jesus are found in all four Gospels.

> Then cometh Jesus from Galilee to Jordan unto John, to be baptized of him. [14]But John forbad him, saying, I have need to be baptized of thee, and comest thou to me? [15]And Jesus answering said unto him, "Suffer it to be so now: for thus it becometh us to fulfil all righteousness." Then he suffered him. [16]And Jesus, when he was baptized, went up straightway out of the water: and, lo, the heavens were opened unto him, and he saw the Spirit of God descending like a dove, and lighting upon him: [17]And lo a voice from heaven, saying, "This is my beloved Son, in whom I am well pleased." (Matthew 3:13–17)

AD 30

Remember, God's law demands an innocent blood sacrifice as payment for the sin of mankind. God, being Spirit, inhabited the body of Jesus giving Jesus the power to stand against all the temptations of satan and stay sinless to the cross. Please also note that since we are justified (just as if we never sinned) by the shed blood of Jesus, we are also saved from God's justice (Great Tribulation). There are many other verses that proclaim the same message!

> "Which of you convinceth me of sin? And if I say the truth, why do ye not believe me?" (John 8:46)

Now!

Therefore being justified by faith, we have peace with God through our Lord Jesus Christ:

> Therefore being justified by faith, we have peace with God through our Lord Jesus Christ: [7]For scarcely for a righteous man will one die: yet peradventure for a good man some would even dare to die. [8]But God commendeth his love toward us, in that, while we were yet sinners, Christ died for us. [9]Much more then, being now justified by his blood, we shall be saved from wrath through him. [10]For if, when we were enemies, we were reconciled to God by the death of his Son, much more, being reconciled, we shall be saved by his life. [11]And not only so, but we also joy in God through our Lord Jesus Christ, by whom we have now received the atonement. (Romans 5:1, 7–11)
>
> And all things are of God, who hath reconciled us to himself by Jesus Christ, and hath given to us the ministry of reconciliation; [19]To wit, that God was in Christ, reconciling the world unto himself, not imputing their trespasses unto them; and hath committed unto us the word of reconciliation. (2 Corinthians 2:18–19)

This next verse recaps that Jesus is to rule and reign forever and ever. Also, Jesus was caught up to heaven and sits on a throne.

> And she brought forth a man child, who was to rule all nations with a rod of iron: and her child was caught up unto God, and to his throne. (Revelation 12:5)
>
> And when he had spoken these things, while they beheld, he was taken up; and a cloud

received him out of their sight. ¹⁰And while they looked steadfastly toward heaven as he went up, behold, two men stood by them in white apparel; ¹¹Which also said, Ye men of Galilee, why stand ye gazing up into heaven? this same Jesus, which is taken up from you into heaven, shall so come in like manner as ye have seen him go into heaven. (Acts 1:9–11)

As explained through all the letters of Paul, Peter, John, and others of the New Testament, you are called to accept the fact that you have sinned and that you need a Savior to be able to stand in the presence of your Creator God with assurance.

As it is written, There is none righteous, no, not one: (Romans 3:10)

For all have sinned, and come short of the glory of God; (Romans 3:23)

For the wages of sin is death; but the gift of God is eternal life through Jesus Christ our Lord. (Romans 6:23)

The Spirit of God fills the entire universe. I believe that God and His love surrounds the nonbeliever and looks for ways to woo them to accept His free gift of salvation through Jesus Christ. When a person accepts God's free gift of salvation, God Himself dwells with you, loves you, and fellowships with you.

Whither shall I go from thy spirit? or whither shall I flee from thy presence? ⁸If I ascend up into heaven, thou art there: if I make my bed in hell, behold, thou art there. ⁹If I take the wings of the morning, and dwell in the uttermost parts of the sea; ¹⁰Even there shall thy hand lead me, and thy right hand shall hold me. (Psalms 139:7–10)

Right now, take a moment before your Creator God, being Spirit, to accept the innocent blood sacrifice of Jesus Christ as your payment for your sins forever by F-A-I-T-H.

> God is a Spirit: and they that worship him must worship him in spirit and in truth. (John 4:24)
> Now faith is the substance of things hoped for, the evidence of things not seen. [6]But without faith it is impossible to please him: for he that cometh to God must believe that he is, and that he is a rewarder of them that diligently seek him. (Hebrews 11:1, 6)

Ask God to come in, fellowship with you, and help you do what He wants you to do.

> Behold, I stand at the door, and knock: if any man hear my voice, and open the door, I will come in to him, and will sup with him, and he with me. (Revelation 3:20)
> What? know ye not that your body is the temple of the Holy Ghost which is in you, which ye have of God, and ye are not your own? (1 Corinthians 6:19)

Too simple? It wasn't simple for Jesus. Just say "thank you" and accept God's totally free gift.

> For by grace are ye saved through faith; and that not of yourselves: it is the gift of God: [9]Not of works, lest any man should boast. (Ephesians 2:8–9)

Afraid of giving up some fun? Don't allow yourself to be deceived. Sin is only fun for a moment, and then sin ultimately brings eternal death. There are always consequences for sin.

But if ye will not do so, behold, ye have sinned against the LORD: and be sure your sin will find you out. (Numbers 32:23)

For the wages of sin is death; but the gift of God is eternal life through Jesus Christ our Lord. (Romans 6:23)

Believe me, your freedom from sin is ultimate joy. God has provided limitless wholesome "fun" things to do that strengthen the spirit within you. Following the Lord Jesus is never boring or empty. Get ready to truly enjoy a "life" of spiritual freedom!

Whom having not seen, ye love; in whom, though now ye see him not, yet believing, ye rejoice with joy unspeakable and full of glory: (1 Peter 1:8)

If you are ready to accept God's free gift of forgiveness, simply take a moment to:

1) Tell God you believe that He exists. Remember, God is all around you in Spirit and He loves you unconditionally.
2) Tell God that you have sinned against Him and that you do not want to sin against Him anymore!
3) Tell God you believe that Jesus died and shed His blood as payment for your sin.
4) Ask God to forgive you of your sin because of what Jesus has done for you.
5) Ask God to come into your life and help you to do what is right.

End all of your prayers with "In the name of Jesus," because the only reason we may pray is because of what Jesus has done for us.

If you have taken this moment to accept God's free gift of salvation for yourself, congratulations and welcome to assurance of eternity with your Creator God.

> These things have I written unto you that believe
> on the name of the Son of God; that ye may know
> that ye have eternal life, and that ye may believe
> on the name of the Son of God. (1 John 5:13)

If you have not, please let it be known that God loves you, and He has made a way of escape for you.

> But God commendeth his love toward us, in
> that, while we were yet sinners, Christ died for
> us. (Romans 5:8)
> That whosoever believeth in him should not
> perish, but have eternal life. [16]For God so loved
> the world, that he gave his only begotten Son,
> that whosoever believeth in him should not per-
> ish, but have everlasting life. [17]For God sent not
> his Son into the world to condemn the world;
> but that the world through him might be saved.
> [18]He that believeth on him is not condemned:
> but he that believeth not is condemned already,
> because he hath not believed in the name of the
> only begotten Son of God. [19]And this is the con-
> demnation, that light is come into the world, and
> men loved darkness rather than light, because
> their deeds were evil. (John 3:15–19)

Hell was created only for satan and the angels that followed him. Please do not force God's hand against you. Jesus Christ shed His innocent blood as payment for all your sins.

> Then shall he say also unto them on the left hand,
> Depart from me, ye cursed, into everlasting fire,

prepared for the devil and his angels: (Matthew 25:41)

Sin is only paid by an innocent blood sacrifice. Since God has come in the form of Jesus Christ to pay for your sin once and for all, Old Testament animal sacrifices will not be sufficient. You must put your faith in what Jesus has accomplished for you on the cross around 30 AD on a hill outside of Jerusalem.

> Jesus saith unto him, I am the way, the truth, and the life: no man cometh unto the Father, but by me. (John 14:6)

The very reason I start every book with the Gospel of Jesus Christ, the way to make yourself right with God, is because God's Spirit, the Comforter, brings to light all truth. If you do not have God's Spirit residing in your heart, it is difficult to understand God's Word. I would like God's Word to be more than just words to you. Even though this book will be interesting and informative, my hope is that the words of this book are fulfilling.

1) What is the first evidence of God's existence? Please give examples.
2) Who allowed sin to enter into God's perfect creation?
3) Write about God's plan to save man from his dreadful mistake of sin? What was the scriptural evidence of the plan?

Memory Verse: Genesis 3:15

1) Why did God make a way for Adam and Eve?

2) Write about the importance of the children of Israel and how miraculous that they still exist today?

3) How did innocent blood save at the time of the original "Passover"? Write about how this event reflects on what Jesus has done for all of us.

Memory Verse: Exodus 12:3

1) How does the story of the Jewish people resemble our own lives?

2) Who is Jesus?

3) Why was it so important that Jesus was born of a virgin?

4) Write about the Christmas story found in Revelation.

Memory Verse: Romans 5:12

1) How did God, Himself, address Jesus?

2) What does "justified" mean?

3) From what does the innocent shed blood of Jesus save us?

4) Write down some thoughts on God's "justice". Another term for "wrath" related to God is justice. God is love and God is just. Sin demands a punishment.

Memory Verse: Romans 5:1

1) What is sin? Have you ever sinned?
2) Why do you need a Savior?
3) What happens when you accept God's free gift of salvation through Jesus Christ?

Memory Verse: Ephesians 2:8,9

1) How do you know if you would go to heaven if you were to die today with no doubts?
2) For who was hell created?
3) Who is condemned?
4) How must sin be paid according to God's justice?
5) Again what is God's simple plan for His creation to enter heaven?

Memory Verse: Romans 6:23

Jesus Is Our Eternal Creator God

Calligraphy Designed By
Maria Grahl
www.wwapbglobal.com
@writewithapurpose

Chapter 2
The Vision

At the time the book of Revelation was written, the Apostle John was the last of the original disciples and banished to a deserted Greek island called Patmos to die with the scorpions. God saved John, so He could show John the future just for you. Jesus, in His glorified body, appeared to John and showed John visions of the twenty-first century. John described what he sees using his first-century knowledge. You need to place yourself in his position to understand what he was seeing.

There is a blessing or happiness for all who read the book of Revelation. God wants to show His creation, His loved ones, and His beloved, what He has for them. God is also a "just" God, and His justice demands punishment to be metered out.

Please reconsider the previous chapter and choose to accept God's escape from this punishment. This book of the future shows us both the glory for the believer and the horrific punishment for the person who refuses God's *free gift* of Salvation.

AD 80

The Revelation of Jesus Christ, which God gave unto him, to shew unto his servants things which must shortly come to pass; and he sent and signified it by his angel unto his servant John: [2]Who bare record of the word of God, and of the testimony of Jesus Christ, and of all things that he

25

saw. ³Blessed is he that readeth, and they that hear the words of this prophecy, and keep those things which are written therein: for the time is at hand. (Revelation 1:1–3)

John is proclaimed as the writer of this book, and it is written to the seven churches of believers in Asia Minor at the time of the writing. God's purpose for this book is to bring grace, peace, and blessings to people who have accepted His free gift of salvation. In a sense, God was showing all of us what we are going to miss by our eternal choice and a glimpse of what we will enjoy!

It seems that each church had its own angel that represents them before God. Please note that we are witnessing the mystery of the Trinity of God or the ability of God to manifest Himself as the Father, the Son, and Holy Spirit at the same time.

With God, known as our Heavenly Father, He took on the body of a baby born to a virgin Mary in Bethlehem of Judea, named Jesus. I do not believe this is the first time Jesus walked with men on earth. I believe the Bible eludes to Jesus, God in human form, first walked with Adam and Eve in the Garden of Eden and, second, spoke with Abraham about Sarah having Isaac with the two angels by His side.

God also comforts each believer with His Holy Spirit who teaches us, comforts us, convicts us, and directs us while living within us. I believe this same Spirit also represents us in the heavens. Talk about a direct connection to our Creator!

John to the seven churches which are in Asia: Grace be unto you, and peace, from him which is, and which was, and which is to come; and from the seven Spirits which are before his throne; ⁵And from Jesus Christ, who is the faithful witness, and the first begotten of the dead, and the prince of the kings of the earth. Unto him that loved us, and washed us from our sins in his own blood, ⁶And hath made us kings and priests unto God and his

Father; to him be glory and dominion for ever and ever. Amen. (Revelation 1:4–6)

A proclamation again of who Jesus is! Jesus is our Eternal Creator God, who came to earth to pay for our sins Himself. Jesus proclaims that He is coming again and this coming refers to the coming at the end of the tribulation period where all will see Him, and the remaining inhabitants will cry because their selfish acts will not be allowed as Jesus, Himself, will rule the earth.

> Behold, he cometh with clouds; and every eye shall see him, and they also which pierced him: and all kindreds of the earth shall wail because of him. Even so, Amen. [8]I am Alpha and Omega, the beginning and the ending, saith the Lord, which is, and which was, and which is to come, the Almighty. [9]I John, who also am your brother, and companion in tribulation, and in the kingdom and patience of Jesus Christ, was in the isle that is called Patmos, for the word of God, and for the testimony of Jesus Christ. (Revelation 1:7–9)

Basically, John was worshipping the Lord on the first day of the week when Jesus appeared to him. Jesus loves his church, and His desire is to have them grow in the wisdom of heaven because He knows they will experience life of inner peace, abundant life! John saw Jesus! What a glorious sight!

> I was in the Spirit on the Lord's day, and heard behind me a great voice, as of a trumpet, [11]Saying, I am Alpha and Omega, the first and the last: and, What thou seest, write in a book, and send it unto the seven churches which are in Asia; unto Ephesus, and unto Smyrna, and unto Pergamos, and unto Thyatira, and unto Sardis, and unto Philadelphia, and unto Laodicea. [12]And I turned

to see the voice that spake with me. And being turned, I saw seven golden candlesticks; ¹³And in the midst of the seven candlesticks one like unto the Son of man, clothed with a garment down to the foot, and girt about the paps with a golden girdle. ¹⁴His head and his hairs were white like wool, as white as snow; and his eyes were as a flame of fire; ¹⁵And his feet like unto fine brass, as if they burned in a furnace; and his voice as the sound of many waters. ¹⁶And he had in his right hand seven stars: and out of his mouth went a sharp two-edged sword: and his countenance was as the sun shineth in his strength. ¹⁷And when I saw him, I fell at his feet as dead. And he laid his right hand upon me, saying unto me, Fear not; I am the first and the last: ¹⁸I am he that liveth, and was dead; and, behold, I am alive for evermore, Amen; and have the keys of hell and of death. ¹⁹Write the things which thou hast seen, and the things which are, and the things which shall be hereafter; ²⁰The mystery of the seven stars which thou sawest in my right hand, and the seven golden candlesticks. The seven stars are the angels of the seven churches: and the seven candlesticks which thou sawest are the seven churches. (Revelation 1:10–20)

The first three chapters of Revelation is where Jesus is showing John a glimpse of heaven and giving messages to the seven churches of Asia Minor or present-day Turkey. These messages are also relevant to believers today. The overall message is to *keep the faith* or *go back to your first love*.

Hold fast to the faith that believes the blood of Jesus Christ alone pays for your sin. Do not follow after any teaching that includes any work of man as part of salvation including baptism, tongues, miracles, etc. Paul told the Galatians that if you add to the blood of

Jesus, you will still be *under the law* and in your sin! Do not fall for the lies of religion!

The Spirit of God who resides in you will guide you into all truth.

> Stand fast therefore in the liberty wherewith Christ hath made us free, and be not entangled again with the yoke of bondage. ²Behold, I Paul say unto you, that if ye be circumcised, Christ shall profit you nothing. ³For I testify again to every man that is circumcised, that he is a debtor to do the whole law. ⁴Christ is become of no effect unto you, whosoever of you are justified by the law; ye are fallen from grace. (Galatians 5:1–4)

> But the Comforter, which is the Holy Ghost, whom the Father will send in my name, he shall teach you all things, and bring all things to your remembrance, whatsoever I have said unto you. (John 14:26)

> Who is a liar but he that denieth that Jesus is the Christ? He is antichrist, that denieth the Father and the Son. ²³Whosoever denieth the Son, the same hath not the Father: (but) he that acknowledgeth the Son hath the Father also. ²⁴Let that therefore abide in you, which ye have heard from the beginning. If that which ye have heard from the beginning shall remain in you, ye also shall continue in the Son, and in the Father. ²⁵And this is the promise that he hath promised us, even eternal life. ²⁶These things have I written unto you concerning them that seduce you. (1 John 2:22–26)

The people of the church in Ephesus were discerning the spirits of the people that called themselves apostles. They did many works and hated sin. I believe they became legalistic in their works and were allowing their works to flood out the fact that God was doing the works through them. The warning is that if they continued, they would eventually worship their works instead of the *one* who performed the works through them.

Jesus was calling them to refocus on Him just like when they first accepted His free gift of salvation. Jesus admired their works but His relationship with them must be put first.

> Unto the angel of the church of Ephesus write; These things saith he that holdeth the seven stars in his right hand, who walketh in the midst of the seven golden candlesticks; ²I know thy works, and thy labour, and thy patience, and how thou canst not bear them which are evil: and thou hast tried them which say they are apostles, and are not, and hast found them liars: ³And hast borne, and hast patience, and for my name's sake hast laboured, and hast not fainted. ⁴Nevertheless I have somewhat against thee, because thou hast left thy first love. ⁵Remember therefore from whence thou art fallen, and repent, and do the first works; or else I will come unto thee quickly, and will remove thy candlestick out of his place, except thou repent. ⁶But this thou hast, that thou hatest the deeds of the Nicolaitans, which I also hate. ⁷He that hath an ear, let him hear what the Spirit saith unto the churches; To him that overcometh will I give to eat of the tree of life, which is in the midst of the paradise of God. (Revelation 2:1–7)

The church in Smyrna was experiencing great persecution just like God's people in certain areas of the world today. Jesus wanted them to know that He saw their tribulation. Jesus let them know that some will face death for their faith in Him. Jesus tried to show them how rich they truly were in heaven. He shows us that if we are faithful, even to death, we will be given a crown of life! Jesus also proclaims that we will escape the second death, lake of fire, created for satan and his demons.

> And unto the angel of the church in Smyrna write; These things saith the first and the last, which was dead, and is alive; ⁹I know thy works, and tribulation, and poverty, (but thou art rich) and I know the blasphemy of them which say they are Jews, and are not, but are the synagogue of satan. ¹⁰Fear none of those things which thou shalt suffer: behold, the devil shall cast some of you into prison, that ye may be tried; and ye shall have tribulation ten days: be thou faithful unto death, and I will give thee a crown of life. ¹¹He that hath an ear, let him hear what the Spirit saith unto the churches; He that overcometh shall not be hurt of the second death. (Revelation 2:8–11)

The church at Pergamos was also experiencing persecution for their faith in Jesus. It seems there are some among them that hold to certain doctrines that oppose the simple Gospel. They were doing things that would cause the people of Israel to refuse the Gospel. It is also evident that some believed they could believe that the blood of Jesus cleanses their sins and continue to live a life of sin.

As a person is convicted of sin by the Holy Spirit, we need to heed the leading of the Holy Spirit and turn from the sin. Certain sins can be difficult to eliminate immediately. God will give you the power to turn as long as your heart's desire is to turn from the sin. Jesus calls the people of the church of Pergamos to *repent* or *desire to turn* from the sin.

Jesus is saying that He would allow hardships to come upon them to turn them from their sin. At this point, either the believer heeds the chastisement of the Lord and continues in the faith, or they turn and harden their heart against the Lord Jesus losing everything.

And to the angel of the church in Pergamos write; These things saith he which hath the sharp sword with two edges; [13]I know thy works, and where thou dwellest, even where Satan's seat is: and thou holdest fast my name, and hast not denied my faith, even in those days wherein Antipas was my faithful martyr, who was slain among you, where satan dwelleth. [14]But I have a few things against thee, because thou hast there them that hold the doctrine of Balaam, who taught Balac to cast a stumblingblock before the children of Israel, to eat things sacrificed unto idols, and to commit fornication. [15]So hast thou also them that hold the doctrine of the Nicolaitans, which thing I hate. [16]Repent; or else I will come unto thee quickly, and will fight against them with the sword of my mouth. [17]He that hath an ear, let him hear what the Spirit saith unto the churches; To him that overcometh will I give to eat of the hidden manna, and will give him a white stone, and in the stone a new name written, which no man knoweth saving he that receiveth it. (Revelation 2:12–17)

The church of Thyatira seems to be the best of all churches from the outside. This church is a giving church with much service and patience. The word "works" is written twice in the same sentence. This church is short on discernment.

The church of Thyatira has allowed a "leader" that is preaching a false message and turning many away from the true Gospel. This church reminds me of the churches today that allow confessing sin in the pulpit, turning their backs on the written Word.

The more a person refuses to acknowledge truth and continue to live a life of sin, eventually, that person will turn from the conviction of the Holy Spirit and turn away from the saving shed blood of the cross of Christ. When a person does not cling to the cross of

Christ and trusts in his own works to please God, he is still under the law and his salvation is lost. Jesus knows your heart!

The person of this church who recognizes the error of the church leaders and holds fast to the truth of the Word will receive a great reward. They will be counted among the Bride of Christ who will rule and rein with Christ over the nations after the Tribulation for a thousand years and into eternity in the "new Heaven" and "new earth!"

> And unto the angel of the church in Thyatira write; These things saith the Son of God, who hath his eyes like unto a flame of fire, and his feet are like fine brass; [19]I know thy works, and charity, and service, and faith, and thy patience, and thy works; and the last to be more than the first. [20]Notwithstanding I have a few things against thee, because thou sufferest that woman Jezebel, which calleth herself a prophetess, to teach and to seduce my servants to commit fornication, and to eat things sacrificed unto idols. [21]And I gave her space to repent of her fornication; and she repented not. [22]Behold, I will cast her into a bed, and them that commit adultery with her into great tribulation, except they repent of their deeds. [23]And I will kill her children with death; and all the churches shall know that I am he which searcheth the reins and hearts: and I will give unto every one of you according to your works. [24]But unto you I say, and unto the rest in Thyatira, as many as have not this doctrine, and which have not known the depths of satan, as they speak; I will put upon you none other burden. [25]But that which ye have already hold fast till I come. [26]And he that overcometh, and keepeth my works unto the end, to him will I give power over the nations: [27]And he shall rule them with a rod of iron; as the

vessels of a potter shall they be broken to shivers: even as I received of my Father. ²⁸And I will give him the morning star. ²⁹He that hath an ear, let him hear what the Spirit saith unto the churches. (Revelation 2:18–29)

The church of Sardis is also a church like Thyatira that looks like a good church on the outside in name alone but has decided to follow the way of the flesh, religion. There are so many false religions that seem to be good but have no spirit within it. This church started with the truth, fell away, repented, and repeated the terrible cycle.

Even in the midst of this church, Jesus has found a few who have not defiled themselves with the false religion. Jesus says they will walk with Him in white! Their names will be secure in the Lamb's Book of Life.

Jesus calls this church to turn from their wicked ways because the rapture, the "snatching away" of the believers, will occur as a thief in the night. Just like the wicked of the church of Thyatira, the people not keeping their faith in the gift of salvation will find themselves in the Tribulation.

And unto the angel of the church in Sardis write; These things saith he that hath the seven Spirits of God, and the seven stars; I know thy works, that thou hast a name that thou livest, and art dead. ²Be watchful, and strengthen the things which remain, that are ready to die: for I have not found thy works perfect before God. ³Remember therefore how thou hast received and heard, and hold fast, and repent. If therefore thou shalt not watch, I will come on thee as a thief, and thou shalt not know what hour I will come upon thee. ⁴Thou hast a few names even in Sardis which have not defiled their garments; and they shall walk with me in white: for they are worthy. ⁵He that overcometh, the same shall be clothed in white raiment; and I will not blot out his name out of the book of life, but I will confess his name before my Father, and before his angels. ⁶He that hath an ear, let him hear what the Spirit saith unto the churches. (Revelation 3:1–6)

The church of Philadelphia has kept the true Gospel in spite of their weaknesses. Jesus is giving them a supernatural love that will be able to reach out to the vilest of sinners. This church is the evangelical church.

Even in all of their work for the Lord Jesus warns them not to allow false prophets, false teachings, worship of their works, or worship of themselves because of the workings of miracles to pull them away from the truth. Jesus proclaims that the people who overcome and endure to the Rapture will never leave His side!

And to the angel of the church in Philadelphia write; These things saith he that is holy, he that is true, he that hath the key of David, he that openeth, and no man shutteth; and shutteth, and no man openeth; ⁸I know thy works: behold, I have set before thee an open door, and no man can shut it: for thou hast a little strength, and hast kept my word, and hast not denied my name. ⁹Behold, I will make them of the synagogue of Satan, which say they are Jews, and are not, but do lie; behold, I will make them to come and worship before thy feet, and to know that I have loved thee. ¹⁰Because thou hast kept the word of my patience, I also will keep thee from the hour of temptation, which shall come upon all the world, to try them that dwell upon the earth. ¹¹Behold, I come quickly: hold that fast which thou hast, that no man take thy crown. ¹²Him that overcometh will I make a pillar in the temple of my God, and he shall go no more out: and I will write upon him the name of my God, and the name of the city of my God, which is new Jerusalem, which cometh down out of heaven from my God: and I will write upon him my new name. ¹³He that hath an ear, let him hear what the Spirit saith unto the churches. (Revelation 3:7–13)

The Laodicean church knows the truth and has become complacent. They have a strong tendency to rely on their own works which is the definition of religion. The religions of the world have heard the truth but are satisfied with their own works to appease God.

Jesus is calling the church of Laodicea to exchange their works (riches) for reliance on God's free gift of the shed blood of Christ. Religion is so blinded by their works that they cannot see their need for a Savior.

Jesus is pictured standing at their door wanting to come in and fellowship with them. God loves them so much, but they must see their need to open their door to Him. Jesus will not open the door. Again, God's creation is in danger of the Tribulation needlessly.

And unto the angel of the church of the Laodiceans write; These things saith the Amen, the faithful and true witness, the beginning of the creation of God; ¹⁵I know thy works, that thou art neither cold nor hot: I would thou wert cold or hot. ¹⁶So then because thou art lukewarm, and neither cold nor hot, I will spue thee out of my mouth. ¹⁷Because thou sayest, I am rich, and increased with goods, and have need of nothing; and knowest not that thou art wretched, and miserable, and poor, and blind, and naked: ¹⁸I counsel thee to buy of me gold tried in the fire, that thou mayest be rich; and white raiment, that thou mayest be clothed, and that the shame of thy nakedness do not appear; and anoint thine eyes with eyesalve, that thou mayest see. ¹⁹As many as I love, I rebuke and chasten: be zealous therefore, and repent. [20]Behold, I stand at the door, and knock: if any man hear my voice, and open the door, I will come in to him, and will sup with him, and he with me. [21]To him that over-cometh will I grant to sit with me in my throne, even as I also overcame, and am set down with my Father in his throne. [22]He that hath an ear, let him hear what the Spirit saith unto the churches. (Revelation 3:14–22)

This is the very reason for chapter 1 of this book. Jesus is calling you to come out from among them if you have not already. Jesus, Almighty God, your Creator God, is calling you to accept His free gift of salvation (being saved from the tribulation and second death).

If you are not absolutely certain you would be with the Lord Jesus if you closed your eyes to the world in the next moment,

We are confident, I say, and willing rather to be absent from the body, and to be present with the Lord. (2 Corinthians 5:8)

Please reconsider and revisit chapter 1 before continuing. I guarantee the rest of this book will bring you peace and joy if you do. The following scriptures are God's plea for you to heed His warnings and desire for you to accept His free gift of forgiveness.

Anytime!
In the future, before the Great Tribulation Period

And he said unto me, These sayings are faithful and true: and the Lord God of the holy prophets sent his angel to shew unto his servants the things which must shortly be done. [7]Behold, I come quickly: blessed is he that keepeth the sayings of the prophecy of this book. [8]And I John saw these things, and heard them. And when I had heard and seen, I fell down to worship before the feet of the angel which shewed me these things. ⁹Then saith he unto me, See thou do it not: for I am thy fellowservant, and of thy brethren the prophets, and of them which keep the sayings of this book: worship God. ¹⁰And he saith unto me, Seal not the sayings of the prophecy of this book: for the time is at hand. ¹¹He that is unjust, let him be unjust still: and he which is filthy, let him be filthy still: and he that is righteous, let him be righteous still: and he that is holy, let him be holy still. ¹²And, behold, I come quickly; and my reward is with me, to give every man according as his work shall be. ¹³I am Alpha and Omega, the beginning and the end, the first and the last. ¹⁴Blessed are they that do his commandments, that they may have right to the tree of life, and may enter in through the gates into the city. ¹⁵For without are dogs, and sorcerers, and whoremongers, and murderers, and idolaters, and whosoever loveth and maketh a lie. ¹⁶I Jesus have sent mine angel to testify unto you these things in the churches. I am the root and the offspring of David, and the bright and morning star. ¹⁷And the Spirit and the bride say, Come. And let him that heareth say, Come. And let him that is athirst come. And whosoever will, let him take the water of life freely. ¹⁸For I testify unto every man that heareth the words of the prophecy of this book, If any man shall add unto these things, God shall add unto him the plagues that are written in this book: ¹⁹And if any man shall take away from the words of the book of this prophecy, God shall take away his part out of the book of life, and out of the holy city, and from the things which are written in this book. ²⁰He which testifieth these things saith,

Surely I come quickly. Amen. Even so, come, Lord Jesus. [21]The grace of our Lord Jesus Christ be with you all. Amen. (Revelation 22:6–21)

1) Who was John? Where was he when God gave him the vision?
2) How must you think when reading about the vision that John saw?
3) What does the book of Revelation show us?
4) For whom did John originally write the Book of Revelation?

Memory Verse: John 14:6

1) What is God's purpose for the Book of Revelation?
2) When was the Book of Revelation written?
3) Write about the Trinity of God, the Father, the Son, and the Holy Spirit?
4) What does the Holy Spirit do for us?

Memory Verse: Revelation 1:3

1) What was John doing when Jesus appeared to him? Write about the importance of what John was doing.
2) What does Alpha and Omega mean? What does it tell us about Jesus?
3) What did Jesus, Himself, say about Himself in verse 18 of Revelation chapter one?
4) What is Jesus showing John and all believers in the first three chapters of Revelation?

5) Hold fast to the faith that believes what? What happens if you do not?

Memory Verse: Galatians 5:1

1) How does the church at Ephesus relate to Christians of today? What did Jesus promise the Ephesus church if they "kept the faith"?
2) How did Jesus encourage the church at Smyrna to "keep the faith" even to the death?
3) As in the church at Pergamos what must we do when the Holy Spirit convicts us of sin?
4) What is happening in today's church that was occurring in the church of Thyatira?
5) As in the church of Sardis why must we be careful not to follow false religions?
6) What is Jesus' caution to the church at Philadelphia?
7) Just like the Laodicean church what must we do to receive Jesus into our life?

Memory Verse: Revelation 3:20

Calligraphy Designed By
Maria Grahl
www.wwapbglobal.com
@writewithapurpose

CHAPTER 3

THE RAPTURE OF THE BELIEVERS

The term "rapture" comes from the Greek "a snatching away" found in Paul's letter to the Thessalonians and Corinthians. The Rapture is also prophesied by Daniel.

ANYTIME!
In the Future
Before the Great Tribulation Period

But I would not have you to be ignorant, brethren, concerning them which are asleep, that ye sorrow not, even as others which have no hope. [14]For if we believe that Jesus died and rose again, even so them also which sleep in Jesus will God bring with him. [15]For this we say unto you by the word of the Lord, that we which are alive and remain unto the coming of the Lord shall not prevent them which are asleep. [16]For the Lord himself shall descend from heaven with a shout, with the voice of the archangel, and with the trump of God: and the dead in Christ shall rise first: [17]Then we which are alive and remain shall be caught up together with them in the clouds, to meet the Lord in the air: and so shall we ever be with the Lord. [18]Wherefore comfort one another with these words. (1 Thessalonians 4:13–18)

Behold, I shew you a mystery; We shall not all sleep, but we shall all be changed, [52]In a moment, in the twinkling of an eye, at the last trump: for the trumpet shall sound, and the dead shall be raised incorruptible, and we shall be changed. [53]For this corruptible must put on incorruption, and this mortal must put on immortality. [54]So when this corruptible shall have put on incorruption, and this mortal shall have put on immortality, then shall be brought to pass the saying that is written, Death is swallowed up in victory. [55]O death, where is thy sting? O grave, where is thy victory? (1 Corinthians 15:51–55)

About 400 BC

And at that time shall Michael stand up, the great prince which standeth for the children of thy people: and there shall be a time of trouble, such as never was since there was a nation even to that same time: and at that time thy people shall be delivered, every one that shall be found written in the book. [2]And many of them that sleep in the dust of the earth shall awake, some to everlasting life, and some to shame and everlasting contempt. [3]And they that be wise shall shine as the brightness of the firmament; and they that turn many to righteousness as the stars for ever and ever. (Daniel 12:1–3)

Prophetic history according to Israel was told to the Old Testament prophet, Daniel. A timetable of seventy weeks of years was appointed to Israel starting at the time Cyrus, King of Persia, gave the decree that Jerusalem could be rebuilt. After 62 weeks of years, 434 years, the "Prince" or Savior, referring to Jesus Christ, was cut off or killed. Another 7 weeks of years, 49 years, was accounted to Israel until Rome destroyed Jerusalem.

> Seventy weeks are determined upon thy people and upon thy holy city, to finish the transgression, and to make an end of sins, and to make reconciliation for iniquity, and to bring in everlasting righteousness, and to seal up the vision and prophecy, and to anoint the most Holy. [25]Know therefore and understand, that from the going forth of the commandment to restore and to build Jerusalem unto the Messiah the Prince shall be seven weeks, and threescore and two weeks: the street shall be built again, and the wall, even in troublous times. [26]And after threescore and two weeks shall Messiah be cut off, but not for himself: and the people of the prince that shall come shall destroy the city and the sanctuary; and the end thereof shall be with a flood, and unto the end of the war desolations are determined. [27]And he shall confirm the covenant with many for one week: and in the midst of the week he shall cause the sacrifice and the oblation to cease, and for the overspreading of abominations he shall make it desolate, even until the consummation, and that determined shall be poured upon the desolate. (Daniel 9:24–27)

Started AD 33
and lasted until the
Rapture of the Church

From the time Jesus was killed until the rapture of the believers is known as the "time of the Gentiles." Jesus called Paul to give the Good News to the Gentiles and this is the reason all mankind is given the gift of salvation through the innocent blood of Jesus Christ. During the "time of the Gentiles," God has given His Spirit to dwell *within* His believers which began at the Feast of Pentecost (fifty days after the death of Jesus and Passover).

The seventieth week of Daniel's vision is a part of Israel's history. The believers are not accounted unto God's justice of the seventieth week. The seventieth week of Daniel's vision is concerning Israel. It is a time of "Jacob's trouble." This moment in history is about God's justice on the evil and ultimately, His effort to bring His chosen Israel back to Him.

> Watch ye therefore, and pray always, that ye may be accounted worthy to escape all these things that shall come to pass, and to stand before the Son of man. (Luke 21:36)

> Much more then, being now justified by his blood, we shall be saved from wrath through him. (Romans 5:9)

> For God hath not appointed us to wrath, but to obtain salvation by our Lord Jesus Christ, [10]Who died for us, that, whether we wake or sleep, we should live together with him. [11]Wherefore comfort yourselves together, and edify one another, even as also ye do. (1 Thessalonians 5:9–11)

ANYTIME!
In the Future
Before the Great Tribulation Period

Since the evil man of perdition, the anti-christ, cannot be revealed until the Holy Spirit is taken out of the way, the believers who have the Holy Spirt residing within must be "snatched away" or *raptured* before the seventieth week begins.

> What? know ye not that your body is the temple of the Holy Ghost which is in you, which ye have of God, and ye are not your own? (1 Corinthians 6:19)

> And grieve not the Holy Spirit of God, whereby ye are sealed unto the day of redemption. (Ephesians 4:30)

> In whom ye also trusted, after that ye heard the word of truth, the gospel of your salvation: in whom also after that ye believed, ye were sealed with that Holy Spirit of promise, (Ephesians 1:13)

> And now ye know what withholdeth that he might be revealed in his time. 7For the mystery of iniquity doth already work: only he who now letteth will let, until he be taken out of the way. 8And then shall that Wicked be revealed, whom the Lord shall consume with the spirit of his mouth, and shall destroy with the brightness of his coming: (2 Thessalonians 2:6–8)

The seventieth week of years, seven years, is described as two halves with a time of peace during the first three and a half year and the time of Great Tribulation during the second half of three and a half years.

I believe the Rapture of the Church is the end of the "time of the Gentiles" or "church age" but does not necessarily begin the "seventieth week clock." The fact that scriptures outline the last week to the exact number of days per the thirty-day per month Jewish calendar is proof that an event will start the "seventieth week clock". I believe this event will be the "peace contract" that will be between Ishmael and Isaac, Esau and Jacob, religious world and Israel.

> And he shall confirm the covenant with many for one week: and in the midst of the week he shall cause the sacrifice and the oblation to cease, and for the overspreading of abominations he shall make it desolate, even until the consummation, and that determined shall be poured upon the desolate. (Daniel 9:27)

I believe the "Rapture of the Church" will occur *before* the "peace treaty" abruptly ending the "church age". Scriptures proclaim that the "rapture" will occur like a "thief in the night". The "rapture of the church" could happen any time since Israel became a nation in 1948.

The garments mentioned in Revelation 16:15 is the seal of the Holy Spirit that saves us from the justice of God. I picture it as if I am covered with the robe of Jesus, covered in His Blood, covering my sin and shame. Cling to the cross! Only the innocent shed blood of Jesus Christ can cleanse your sin and make you sinless and worthy to be in God's presence. Accept no substitute! God does not!

> But of the times and the seasons, brethren, ye have no need that I write unto you. ²For yourselves know perfectly that the day of the Lord so cometh as a thief in the night. (1 Thessalonians 5:1–2)

> Behold, I come as a thief. Blessed is he that watcheth, and keepeth his garments, lest he walk naked, and they see his shame. (Revelation 16:15)

Please note that Jesus talks about the Tribulation Period first in Matthew 24. Verse 35 is a pause proclaiming that the previous prophecy was faithful and true. Jesus then continues to talk about the Rapture.

> But of that day and hour knoweth no man, no, not the angels of heaven, but my Father only. [37]But as the days of Noe were, so shall also the coming of the Son of man be. [38]For as in the days that were before the flood they were eating and drinking, marrying and giving in marriage, until the day that Noe entered into the ark, [39]And knew not until the flood came, and took them all away; so shall also the coming of the Son of man be. [40]Then shall two be in the field; the one shall be taken, and the other left. [41]Two women shall be grinding at the mill; the one shall be taken, and the other left. [42]Watch therefore: for ye know not what hour your Lord doth come. (Matthew 24:36–42)

> And as it was in the days of Noe, so shall it be also in the days of the Son of man. [27]They did eat, they drank, they married wives, they were given in marriage, until the day that Noe entered into the ark, and the flood came, and destroyed them all. [28]Likewise also as it was in the days of Lot; they did eat, they drank, they bought, they sold, they planted, they builded; [29]But the same day that Lot went out of Sodom it rained fire and brimstone from heaven, and destroyed them all. [30]Even thus shall it be in the day when the Son of man is revealed. [31]In that day, he which shall be upon the housetop, and his stuff in the house, let him not come down to take it away: and he that is in the field, let him likewise not return back.

³²Remember Lot's wife. ³³Whosoever shall seek to save his life shall lose it; and whosoever shall lose his life shall preserve it. ³⁴I tell you, in that night there shall be two men in one bed; the one shall be taken, and the other shall be left. ³⁵Two women shall be grinding together; the one shall be taken, and the other left. ³⁶Two men shall be in the field; the one shall be taken, and the other left. (Luke 17:26–36)

In verse 6 of chapter 20, the Rapture is the "first resurrection." In 4:1, a loud voice, like a trumpet, calls the believers to "come up hither." It says, "a door is opened in heaven," and remember that Jesus was referred to as the "door" in the scripture where no man may enter heaven except through Him.

After this I looked, and, behold, a door was opened in heaven: and the first voice which I heard was as it were of a trumpet talking with me; which said, Come up hither, and I will shew thee things which must be hereafter. (Revelation 4:1)

Blessed and holy is he that hath part in the first resurrection: on such the second death hath no power, but they shall be priests of God and of Christ, and shall reign with him a thousand years. (Revelation 20:6)

Then said Jesus unto them again, Verily, verily, I say unto you, I am the door of the sheep. ⁹I am the door: by me if any man enter in, he shall be saved, and shall go in and out, and find pasture. (John 10:7, 9)

1) The word "rapture" is not found in the Bible but what does the word mean?

2) How many years represents the "sixty-two weeks of years"?
3) Describe the "Times of the Gentiles".
4) When did the Holy Spirit begin to dwell within the believer?

Memory Verse: Romans 5:9

1) What is the main purpose of the seventieth week of Daniel's vision or Great Tribulation Period?
2) Who is prohibiting the anti-christ from appearing? What must happen and why?
3) Describe the two halves of the seven year period. What brings the "Time of the Gentiles" or "Church Age" to a close.
4) What event starts the "seventieth week" clock and why?

Memory Verse: 1 Thessalonians 5:9

1) What is the term associated with the "rapture" because it comes unexpectedly?
2) Describe what the garments of Revelation 16:15 mean?
3) Explain how you must read the teaching of Jesus in Matthew 24.
4) In verse 6 of Revelation 20 the rapture is known as what? Explain the reference to a "door" and what it means.

Memory Verse: John 10:9

God
wants you
to
Understand

Calligraphy Designed By
Maria Grahl
www.wwapbglobal.com
@ @writewithapurpose

CHAPTER 4
GOD'S WAY UNDERSTOOD

We see the seventh angel of chapter 10 giving a book to John. The book is sweet at first: portraying the sweetness of peace, symbolizing the peace contract the world would give Israel. The bitterness of the book portrays the breaking of the peace, the persecution of the antichrist, and the justice of God during the last three and a half years of the Tribulation Period.

John is called to prophesy *again* concerning the seven-year period, chapters 11 through 16. As you look at the book of Revelation, you will see that God shows John multiple versions of the same events to help you understand the events. Please also understand that God shows you what is going on in Heaven during this time as well as what is happening on earth.

God often retells events to give mankind another perspective to see His truth in a fuller, real way. One example is the Pharaoh's dreams that Joseph interpreted. There were two dreams and only one event. Jesus told many different parables about Heaven and hell to help you understand.

Revelation is no different. God wants you to understand the book of Revelation and be ready for His return.

> And the voice which I heard from heaven spake unto me again, and said, Go and take the little book which is open in the hand of the angel which standeth upon the sea and upon the earth. ⁹And I went unto the angel, and said unto him, Give me

the little book. And he said unto me, Take it, and eat it up; and it shall make thy belly bitter, but it shall be in thy mouth sweet as honey. [10]And I took the little book out of the angel's hand, and ate it up; and it was in my mouth sweet as honey: and as soon as I had eaten it, my belly was bitter. [11]And he said unto me, Thou must prophesy again before many peoples, and nations, and tongues, and kings. (Revelation 10:8–11)

1) What is the meaning of the book that the angel instructs John to eat?
2) Why does God have John write about the same event twice?
3) Why is it important to know what is happening in heaven and on earth during this seven year period?

Memory Verse: 1 Corinthians 6:19

Eternity will be Amazing

Calligraphy Designed By
Maria Grahl
www.wwapbglobal.com
@writewithapurpose

CHAPTER 5
THE SEALED SAINTS IN HEAVEN

In Heaven
Shortly after the Rapture of the Church

The believers (saints) are now sealed and safe from God's justice in Heaven with Jesus. Chapter 7 is the famous chapter talking about the 144,000 that are sealed. Immediately after mentioning the 144,000, we see verse 9 proclaim a "great multitude, which no man can number" before the Lamb (Jesus) and clothed in "white robes" of righteousness.

I believe that the counts are believers in Jesus, their Messiah, from the twelve tribes of Israel taken in the Rapture of the Church. They are sealed by the Holy Spirit just as the Gentile believers. I also believe the 144,000 is to mean "many" and not an actual number, but I leave this detail to God. I believe this is a time before the "judgement seat" of Christ.

In verse 14, the words "came out of great tribulation" does not necessarily mean that the believers came out of the time the theologians have named the Great Tribulation. All believers throughout the ages have and will face great tribulation keeping their faith in the Gospel of Jesus Christ. Many have and will die for their faith.

As verse 16 proclaims, "eternity will be amazing where we will hunger or thirst no more." Jesus, our bridegroom, will provide all that we need!

> And after these things I saw four angels standing on
> the four corners of the earth, holding the four winds

of the earth, that the wind should not blow on the earth, nor on the sea, nor on any tree. [2]And I saw another angel ascending from the east, having the seal of the living God: and he cried with a loud voice to the four angels, to whom it was given to hurt the earth and the sea, [3]Saying, Hurt not the earth, neither the sea, nor the trees, till we have sealed the servants of our God in their foreheads. [4]And I heard the number of them which were sealed: and there were sealed an hundred and forty and four thousand of all the tribes of the children of Israel. [5]Of the tribe of Juda were sealed twelve thousand. Of the tribe of Reuben were sealed twelve thousand. Of the tribe of Gad were sealed twelve thousand. [6]Of the tribe of Aser were sealed twelve thousand. Of the tribe of Nepthalim were sealed twelve thousand. Of the tribe of Manasses were sealed twelve thousand. [7]Of the tribe of Simeon were sealed twelve thousand. Of the tribe of Levi were sealed twelve thousand. Of the tribe of Issachar were sealed twelve thousand. [8]Of the tribe of Zabulon were sealed twelve thousand. Of the tribe of Joseph were sealed twelve thousand. Of the tribe of Benjamin were sealed twelve thousand. [9]After this I beheld, and, lo, a great multitude, which no man could number, of all nations, and kindreds, and people, and tongues, stood before the throne, and before the Lamb, clothed with white robes, and palms in their hands; [10] And cried with a loud voice, saying, Salvation to our God which sitteth upon the throne, and unto the Lamb. [11]And all the angels stood round about the throne, and about the elders and the four beasts, and fell before the throne on their faces, and worshipped God, [12]Saying, Amen: Blessing, and glory, and wisdom, and thanksgiving, and honour, and power, and might, be unto our God for ever and ever. Amen.

[13]And one of the elders answered, saying unto me, What are these which are arrayed in white robes? and whence came they? [14]And I said unto him, Sir, thou knowest. And he said to me, These are they which came out of great tribulation, and have washed their robes, and made them white in the blood of the Lamb. [15]Therefore are they before the throne of God, and serve him day and night in his temple: and he that sitteth on the throne shall dwell among them. [16]They shall hunger no more, neither thirst anymore; neither shall the sun light on them, nor any heat. [17]For the Lamb which is in the midst of the throne shall feed them, and shall lead them unto living fountains of waters: and God shall wipe away all tears from their eyes. (Revelation 7:1–17)

Chapter 14 talks about the same 144,000 as being the first fruits of the believers. This is clearly talking about the multitude of believers that have arrived during the rapture and found blameless! The believers are not blameless because of what they have done. They are blameless because the blood shed by Jesus Christ has paid for and covered their sins.

Revelation proclaims that these believers have not defiled themselves with women and are virgins. We must understand once and for all that when God washes all your sin away and makes you perfectly sinless, He really means that you are without sin. God proclaims that very fact about you in chapter 14 below.

We also see that God is sending angels to earth to preach the Gospel of Jesus Christ on earth since the believers with the Holy Spirit have been taken out of the way in the rapture. These heavenly messengers are going before the two human prophets that come on the scene about the thirty-third month.

And I looked, and, lo, a Lamb stood on the mount Sion, and with him an hundred forty and four thousand, having his Father's name written in their foreheads. [2]And I heard a voice from heaven, as the voice of many waters, and as the voice of a great thunder: and I heard the voice of harpers harping with their harps: ³And they sung as it were a new song before the throne, and before the four beasts, and the elders: and no man could learn that song but the hundred and forty and four thousand, which were redeemed from the earth. ⁴These are they which were not defiled with women; for they are virgins. These are they which follow the Lamb whithersoever he goeth. These were redeemed from among men, being the firstfruits unto God and to the Lamb. ⁵And in their mouth was found no guile: for they are without fault before the throne of God. ⁶And I saw another angel fly in the midst of heaven, having the everlasting gospel to preach unto them that dwell on the earth, and to every nation, and kindred, and tongue, and people, ⁷Saying with a loud voice, Fear God, and give glory to him; for the hour of his judgment is come: and worship him that made heaven, and earth, and the sea, and the fountains of waters. (Revelation 14:1–7)

Chapter 4 of Revelation explains events in Heaven right after the rapture of the believers. Raptured saints are given positions in Heaven because of their works on earth.

This is a major reason for being conscious of doing good works after salvation. We, the bride, will be blessed with rewards and positions in Heaven for the "thousand-year-reign on earth" as well as for eternity in the "new Heaven" and "new earth" with Jesus, our bridegroom. Do not neglect doing what is right. Remember, it is never wrong to do what is right!

For we must all appear before the judgment seat of Christ; that every one may receive the things done in his body, according to that he hath done, whether it be good or bad. (2 Corinthians 5:10)

And immediately I was in the spirit: and, behold, a throne was set in heaven, and one sat on the throne. [3]And he that sat was to look upon like a jasper and a sardine stone: and there was a rainbow round about the throne, in sight like unto an emerald. [4]And round about the throne were four and twenty seats: and upon the seats I saw four and twenty elders sitting, clothed in white raiment; and they had on their heads crowns of gold. [5]And out of the throne proceeded lightnings and thunderings and voices: and there were seven lamps of fire burning before the throne, which are the seven Spirits of God. [6]And before the throne there was a sea of glass like unto crystal: and in the midst of the throne, and round about the throne, were four beasts full of eyes before and behind. [7]And the first beast was like a lion, and the second beast like a calf, and the third beast had a face as a man, and the fourth beast was like a flying eagle. [8]And the four beasts had each of them six wings about him; and they were full of eyes within: and they rest not day and night, saying, Holy, holy, holy, Lord God Almighty, which was, and is, and is to come. [9]And when those beasts give glory and honour and thanks to him that sat on the throne, who liveth for ever and ever, (Revelation 4:2–9)

Some saints are saved as by fire as they did not do very much to further the kingdom. I, for one, would not want to be embarrassed in front of the multitudes in Heaven without anything to show for my time as a Christian.

If any man's work shall be burned, he shall suffer loss: but he himself shall be saved; yet so as by fire. (1 Corinthians 3:15)

This seems to be moments after the "judgement seat" of Christ in Heaven.

> The four and twenty elders fall down before him that sat on the throne, and worship him that liveth for ever and ever, and cast their crowns before the throne, saying, [11]Thou art worthy, O Lord, to receive glory and honour and power: for thou hast created all things, and for thy pleasure they are and were created. (Revelation 4:10–11)

1) What is mentioned immediately after the mention of the 144,000? How does this help our understanding?
2) What does God do with our sins? Why must this be accomplished? Explain what this means to you.
3) Why should we as "saved believers" strive to do what God calls us to be doing?
4) What happens to our bad deeds done after we put our faith in the shed blood of Jesus as payment for our sins?

Memory Verse: 1 Corinthians 3:15

Peace
is Broken

When the time
is

Right

Calligraphy Designed By
Maria Grahl
www.wwapbglobal.com
@writewithapurpose

CHAPTER 6
THE BEGINNING OF PEACE ON EARTH

On Earth
Month 1–42
(first half of three and a half years)

After the Holy Spirit is taken out of the way by the rapture of the believers, in whom the Holy Spirit of God dwells, several important events will be allowed to occur.

Religions of the world will be allowed to come together under one banner except Judaism which has been shunned and persecuted from the time Rome destroyed Jerusalem around AD 70. This ecumenical fusion of the religions has been occurring and will continue to take place well before the Rapture and will be allowed to culminate after the Rapture.

The religions of the world will be used by the antichrist and the false prophet to gain the worship of the world and access to the temple of Jerusalem to proclaim himself as god. The antichrist knows he cannot accomplish this without a false peace. This method of creating peace to ultimately conquer has been executed before in history.

I believe this world leader will now convince the world as a whole to make peace with Israel and, thus, the "peace contract" that will set in motion the "seventieth week clock" of the vision of the prophet Daniel. The temple will be allowed to be built, and Israel will be allowed to worship during this time until the peace contract is broken. Now we already know from history that a "peace contract" to some is only a "cease-fire". When the time is right, the peace will be broken.

In Heaven
Month 1
And Beyond

Jesus is the only one able to unleash the Great Tribulation trials to bring the end of time because He faced temptation without sin. John was frightened when he learned that nobody was able to open the book in the vision. One of the elders came forward and calmed John saying, "There is One, the Lamb of God, Jesus." Only He is worthy to open the book.

Since Jesus, the Lamb of God, is the only person who is able to open the seals of the Great Tribulation Period, and the first seal deals with the period of false peace, we must look at these verses of chapter 5 right after the Rapture occurs.

> And I saw in the right hand of him that sat on the throne a book written within and on the backside, sealed with seven seals. ²And I saw a strong angel proclaiming with a loud voice, Who is worthy to open the book, and to loose the seals thereof? ³And no man in heaven, nor in earth, neither under the earth, was able to open the book, neither to look thereon. ⁴And I wept much, because no man was found worthy to open and to read the book, neither to look thereon. ⁵And one of the elders saith unto me, Weep not: behold, the Lion of the tribe of Juda, the Root of David, hath prevailed to open the book, and to loose the seven seals thereof. ⁶And I beheld, and, lo, in the midst of the throne and of the four beasts, and in the midst of the elders, stood a Lamb as it had been slain, having seven horns and seven eyes, which are the seven Spirits of God sent forth into all the earth. ⁷And he came and took the

book out of the right hand of him that sat upon the throne. [8]And when he had taken the book, the four beasts and four and twenty elders fell down before the Lamb, having every one of them harps, and golden vials full of odours, which are the prayers of saints. (Revelation 5:1–8)

Jesus opens the book then starts the "seventieth week clock" in Heaven, and this event coincides with the signing of the "peace contract" on earth. All of heaven are in awe at the sight of the Lamb of God, Jesus, and are in a state of worship.

These verses talk about these saints casting their crowns before the throne of God. The twenty-four elders seem to represent the leaders of the ten thousand times ten thousand mentioned in Rev 5:11.

This scripture also confirms again that the saints saved from God's justice (Great Tribulation), a part of Daniel's vision and a time appointed to Israel's calendar, are in Heaven before the Great Tribulation begins. The saints are already there and have experienced the "judgement seat" of Christ because they have their crowns. Verse 10 proclaims that Jesus has made them kings and priests to reign on the earth. Angels have not been given this promise.

And they sung a new song, saying, Thou art worthy to take the book, and to open the seals thereof: for thou wast slain, and hast redeemed us to God by thy blood out of every kindred, and tongue, and people, and nation; [10]And hast made us unto our God kings and priests: and we shall reign on the earth. [11]And I beheld, and I heard the voice of many angels round about the throne and the beasts and the elders: and the number of them was ten thousand times ten thousand, and thousands of thousands; [12]Saying with a loud voice, Worthy is the Lamb that was slain to receive power, and riches, and wisdom, and strength, and honour, and glory, and blessing.

> [13]And every creature which is in heaven, and on
> the earth, and under the earth, and such as are in
> the sea, and all that are in them, heard I saying,
> Blessing, and honour, and glory, and power, be
> unto him that sitteth upon the throne, and unto
> the Lamb for ever and ever. [14]And the four beasts
> said, Amen. And the four and twenty elders fell
> down and worshipped him that liveth for ever
> and ever. (Revelation 5:9–14)

Please note that the one sitting on the white horse of the first
seal has a bow but no arrows. He is also set up as a king or great
leader, symbolizing the crown on his head. He goes forth to conquer
with a false peace.

The antichrist calms concerns revolving around the Christians
taken in the Rapture. He calms warring between Israel and her enemies. He also brings together the religions of the world for peace.

> And I saw when the Lamb opened one of the
> seals, and I heard, as it were the noise of thun-
> der, one of the four beasts saying, Come and see.
> [2]And I saw, and behold a white horse: and he that
> sat on him had a bow; and a crown was given
> unto him: and he went forth conquering, and to
> conquer. (Revelation 6:1–2)

On Earth
Month 1–42
(first half of three and a half years)

The beginning of Revelation chapter 11 describes for us the
temple that will be built so the Jewish people will again worship as
they did in the Old Testament in Jerusalem during the time of peace
and safety.

And there was given me a reed like unto a rod:
and the angel stood, saying, Rise, and measure
the temple of God, and the altar, and them that
worship therein. [2]But the court which is without the temple leave out, and measure it not; for
it is given unto the Gentiles: and the holy city
shall they tread under foot forty and two months.
(Revelation 11:1–2)

The woman (Jewish people) is given sanctuary or peace which
lasts 1,260 days or half of the seventieth week. I assume the peace
contract itself was meant to be "ongoing and never-ending". Jesus
proclaims that the peace will be broken after precisely 1,260 days
after it is signed. The 1,260 days translates into exactly 42 months or
three and a half years by the thirty-day Jewish calendar.

And the woman fled into the wilderness, where
she hath a place prepared of God, that they
should feed her there a thousand two hundred
and threescore days. (Revelation 12:6)

560 BC
Date of Daniel's Vision

The first verse of chapter 13 talks about the antichrist right after
the Rapture of the Church has occurred. Many times, this person
is thought to come out of the original ten-nation European Union
known as the Revived Roman Empire or the "ten toes of iron and
clay" of King Nebuchadnezzar's vision that Daniel interpreted.

The king answered and said to Daniel, whose
name was Belteshazzar, Art thou able to make
known unto me the dream which I have seen,
and the interpretation thereof? [27]Daniel answered
in the presence of the king, and said, The secret
which the king hath demanded cannot the wise

men, the astrologers, the magicians, the soothsay-
ers, shew unto the king; [28]But there is a God in
heaven that revealeth secrets, and maketh known
to the king Nebuchadnezzar what shall be in the
latter days. Thy dream, and the visions of thy head
upon thy bed, are these; [29]As for thee, O king,
thy thoughts came into thy mind upon thy bed,
what should come to pass hereafter: and he that
revealeth secrets maketh known to thee what shall
come to pass. [30]But as for me, this secret is not
revealed to me for any wisdom that I have more
than any living, but for their sakes that shall make
known the interpretation to the king, and that
thou mightest know the thoughts of thy heart.
[31]Thou, O king, sawest, and behold a great image.
This great image, whose brightness was excellent,
stood before thee; and the form thereof was terrible. [32]This image's head was of fine gold, his breast
and his arms of silver, his belly and his thighs of
brass, [33]His legs of iron, his feet part of iron and
part of clay. [34]Thou sawest till that a stone was cut
out without hands, which smote the image upon
his feet that were of iron and clay, and brake them
to pieces. [35]Then was the iron, the clay, the brass,
the silver, and the gold, broken to pieces together,
and became like the chaff of the summer thresh-
ingfloors; and the wind carried them away, that no
place was found for them: and the stone that smote
the image became a great mountain, and filled the
whole earth. [36]This is the dream; and we will tell
the interpretation thereof before the king. [37]Thou,
O king, art a king of kings: for the God of heaven
hath given thee a kingdom, power, and strength,
and glory. [38]And wheresoever the children of men
dwell, the beasts of the field and the fowls of the
heaven hath he given into thine hand, and hath

made thee ruler over them all. Thou art this head of gold. [39]And after thee shall arise another kingdom inferior to thee, and another third kingdom of brass, which shall bear rule over all the earth. [40]And the fourth kingdom shall be strong as iron: forasmuch as iron breaketh in pieces and subdueth all things: and as iron that breaketh all these, shall it break in pieces and bruise. [41]And whereas thou sawest the feet and toes, part of potters' clay, and part of iron, the kingdom shall be divided; but there shall be in it of the strength of the iron, forasmuch as thou sawest the iron mixed with miry clay. [42]And as the toes of the feet were part of iron, and part of clay, so the kingdom shall be partly strong, and partly broken. [43]And whereas thou sawest iron mixed with miry clay, they shall mingle themselves with the seed of men: but they shall not cleave one to another, even as iron is not mixed with clay. [44]And in the days of these kings shall the God of heaven set up a kingdom, which shall never be destroyed: and the kingdom shall not be left to other people, but it shall break in pieces and consume all these kingdoms, and it shall stand for ever. [45]Forasmuch as thou sawest that the stone was cut out of the mountain without hands, and that it brake in pieces the iron, the brass, the clay, the silver, and the gold; the great God hath made known to the king what shall come to pass hereafter: and the dream is certain, and the interpretation thereof sure. (Daniel 2:26–45)

The beast also has more than one head. I believe the political beast (the main figurehead) does come out of the European Union and is linked to a movement to create a worldwide government and religion. The spiritual head of the beast will come on the scene around the time that the peace (cease fire) is broken in the forty-third month.

On Earth
Month 1–42
(first half of three and a half years)

> And I stood upon the sand of the sea, and saw a beast rise up out of the sea, having seven heads and ten horns, and upon his horns ten crowns, and upon his heads the name of blasphemy. (Revelation 13:1)

> And I beheld another beast coming up out of the earth; and he had two horns like a lamb, and he spake as a dragon. 12 And he exerciseth all the power of the first beast before him, and causeth the earth and them which dwell therein to worship the first beast, whose deadly wound was healed. (Revelation 13:11,12)

As mentioned earlier, worldwide religion comes together to join an alliance for peace, and the beginning of chapter 17 explains the great whore (religion) that rides the beast, the antichrist. The beast uses the great whore to draw men away from the truth of God. Religion has been doing just that from the very beginning with satan as its author.

It is proclaimed that the great whore comes from the city that sits on seven hills. The woman rides the "red-colored beast" with ten horns and seven heads. Religion itself has killed more people in the name of god than any war throughout history.

Religion will be destroyed later and will be explained to you shortly.

> And there came one of the seven angels which had the seven vials, and talked with me, saying unto me, Come hither; I will shew unto thee the

judgment of the great whore that sitteth upon many waters: ²With whom the kings of the earth have committed fornication, and the inhabitants of the earth have been made drunk with the wine of her fornication. ³So he carried me away in the spirit into the wilderness: and I saw a woman sit upon a scarlet coloured beast, full of names of blasphemy, having seven heads and ten horns. ⁴And the woman was arrayed in purple and scarlet colour, and decked with gold and precious stones and pearls, having a golden cup in her hand full of abominations and filthiness of her fornication: ⁵And upon her forehead was a name written, MYSTERY, BABYLON THE GREAT, THE MOTHER OF HARLOTS AND ABOMINATIONS OF THE EARTH. ⁶And I saw the woman drunken with the blood of the saints, and with the blood of the martyrs of Jesus: and when I saw her, I wondered with great admiration. ⁷And the angel said unto me, Wherefore didst thou marvel? I will tell thee the mystery of the woman, and of the beast that carrieth her, which hath the seven heads and ten horns. (Revelation 17:1–7)

And here is the mind which hath wisdom. The seven heads are seven mountains, on which the woman sitteth. (Revelation 17:9)

On Earth
Month 34

Verses 3 through 6 of chapter 11 speak about the two witnesses who proclaim the Gospel as prophets did in the Old Testament as this period is now under the Old Testament, the last week of years (seven years) as in Daniel's vision. Some believe these two prophets to be Elijah and Enoch, who are the only humans never to taste death.

The Holy Spirit does not inhabit mankind as during the "time of the Gentiles."

> What? know ye not that your body is the temple of the Holy Ghost which is in you, which ye have of God, and ye are not your own? (1 Corintians 6:19)

During the tribulation period God speaks only through certain people at certain times as in the Old Testament. The two prophets are protected by God to witness on the earth for 1,260 days which is forty-two months according to the thirty-day Jewish calendar. The "time of peace" is also forty-two months or three and a half years. Again the "time of peace" is the first half of the tribulation period beginning with the signing of the peace contract. The Jews are able to worship in the temple that is to be built during the "time of peace".

I believe the two time periods of 1,260 days mentioned above are the same length of time but occur at different periods during the tribulation time. I believe God's two witnesses come on the scene during month thirty-four or toward the end of the "time of peace". These two men will ramp up God's convictions and God's message to the people. In a sense, these two men will be the fuse that causes the antichrist to end the "peace contract" and, eventually, take his place in the Jewish temple in Jerusalem.

> And I will give power unto my two witnesses, and they shall prophesy a thousand two hundred and threescore days, clothed in sackcloth. ⁴These are the two olive trees, and the two candlesticks standing before the God of the earth. ⁵And if any man will hurt them, fire proceedeth out of their mouth, and devoureth their enemies: and if any man will hurt them, he must in this manner be killed. ⁶These have power to shut heaven, that it

71

rain not in the days of their prophecy: and have power over waters to turn them to blood, and to smite the earth with all plagues, as often as they will. (Revelation 11:3–6)

1) Explain why the believers must be taken in the rapture?
2) How will the religions of the world be used by the anti-christ after the rapture?
3) What will Israel be allowed to do after the peace contract?
4) Why is Jesus the only one who can allow the Great Tribulation period to begin?
5) What happens on earth when Jesus opens the book in heaven?

Memory Verse: Revelation 20:6

1) What do the saints do when Jesus, their Bridegroom, opens the book? Why is this important to timing of the rapture of the believers?
2) The first seal portrays the anti-christ riding a white horse and what does this mean?
3) How long will the peace last and what will happen when it is broken
4) What year did Daniel interpret the vision for King Nebuchadnezzar? How does this vision relate to the anti-christ?

Memory Verse: John 3:16-17

1) How many people make up the "beast"? Describe both individuals.
2) How is the one-world religion portrayed in chapter 17? How does the anti-christ use the one-world religion?
3) Consider all of the different religions and how they in one way or another add to the "cross" or divert away from the "cross". Write down your thoughts.

Memory Verse: John 3:18

1) Who are the two human witnesses or prophets who come on the scene around week 34? Why do we believe this to be a possibility?
2) How does the Holy Spirt work during the "seventieth week"?
3) What is the purpose of the two witnesses?
4) What is the significance of the two witnesses on the anti-christ?

Memory Verse: 1 John 5:13

Prayers
are
Definitely
Heard

Calligraphy Designed By
Maria Grahl
www.wwapbglobal.com
@writewithapurpose

CHAPTER 7
THE BEGINNING OF THE END

On Earth
Month 43–44

The seventh seal was opened which seemed to signal the angels with the seven trumpets. At this point, I believe God is giving us a more detailed version of the last moments of the Tribulation Period. There was silence or peace for half an hour. This could relate to the peace for half the time of the period of seven years appointed unto Israel. The remaining trumpets and bowls describe *again* the "justice of the Lamb."

The prayers of the saints could mean the prayers of all the saints through the ages because of persecutions and tribulations caused by the evils of the demonic realm. The demonic realm works through men to pour out trials and tribulations on the saints. Their prayers were and are definitely heard.

> And when he had opened the seventh seal, there was silence in heaven about the space of half an hour. ²And I saw the seven angels which stood before God; and to them were given seven trumpets. ³And another angel came and stood at the altar, having a golden censer; and there was given unto him much incense, that he should offer it with the prayers of all saints upon the golden altar which was before the throne. ⁴And the smoke of

the incense, which came with the prayers of the saints, ascended up before God out of the angel's hand. ⁵And the angel took the censer, and filled it with fire of the altar, and cast it into the earth: and there were voices, and thunderings, and lightnings, and an earthquake. ⁶And the seven angels which had the seven trumpets prepared themselves to sound. (Revelation 8:1–6)

The anti-christ, now with a great sword, comes to take peace from the earth. This occurs around the forty-third month. Declaration of the "mark of the beast" begins at this time which could possibly be an RFID (radio-frequency identification) personal identification chip that is made a requirement to buy or sell. Another possible mark may be the devotion to the worldwide government and religion.

And when he had opened the second seal, I heard the second beast say, Come and see. ⁴And there went out another horse that was red: and power was given to him that sat thereon to take peace from the earth, and that they should kill one another: and there was given unto him a great sword. (Revelation 6:3–4)

1) All prayers are heard. How do the events in the scriptures show us to have patience in God's perfect timing? Talk about examples in your life.

2) What are the two possibilities for the "mark of the beast"? Offer other suggestions or possibilities.

3) What color is the horse of the anti-christ after breaking the peace and what are the differences when he rode the white horse?

Memory Verse: Psalms 119:11

Men
Deceived
By the Power
of the
antichrist

Calligraphy Designed By
Maria Grahl
www.wwapbglobal.com
@ @writewithapurpose

CHAPTER 8
THE REAL ANTICHRIST

On Earth
Month 43–76

The antichrist is able to do amazing works convincing mankind that remain that he is god. The antichrist begins to persecute the Jewish people and people who refuse to follow his commands. This is where the Tribulation Saints, who finally saw the truth, refuse to take the "mark." These people are killed by beheading. People will not be able to buy or sell unless they have the "mark."

> And when he had opened the third seal, I heard the third beast say, Come and see. And I beheld, and lo a black horse; and he that sat on him had a pair of balances in his hand. 6And I heard a voice in the midst of the four beasts say, A measure of wheat for a penny, and three measures of barley for a penny; and see thou hurt not the oil and the wine. (Revelation 6:5–6)

> And I saw thrones, and they sat upon them, and judgment was given unto them: and I saw the souls of them that were beheaded for the witness of Jesus, and for the word of God, and which had not worshipped the beast, neither his image, neither had received his mark upon their foreheads,

or in their hands; and they lived and reigned with
Christ a thousand years. (Revelation 20:4)

Around month forty-four or forty-five, the political antichrist
suffers a deadly blow and is healed which made the world wonder
and begin to worship him. The devil is giving the political antichrist
his power to do these wonders. About this time, the religious antichrist emerges on the scene. This power comes into the open to point
all people to worship the *political* antichrist as a god. The *religious*
antichrist proclaims that no one will be able to buy or sell without
the "mark."

This person has fire rain from Heaven and does many supernatural things. Men are deceived by his powers. I now believe this
"mark" may very well be a mark that designates that the person is a
worshipper of the worldwide religion.

The dragon is satan, and the beast is the political antichrist,
who is wounded and healed, and the religious beast directs worship
to the political antichrist.

During the next few months is when the people who do not
bow down and worship the beast will be beheaded. Remember also
that God's two witnesses are also still proclaiming the Gospel of Jesus
with power protecting them from harm until their time was finished
about the seventy-sixth month.

Verse 7 and 8 refers to how difficult it will be for people who
come to faith during the Tribulation Period.

> And the beast which I saw was like unto a leop-
> ard, and his feet were as the feet of a bear, and his
> mouth as the mouth of a lion: and the dragon gave
> him his power, and his seat, and great authority.
> ³And I saw one of his heads as it were wounded
> to death; and his deadly wound was healed: and
> all the world wondered after the beast. ⁴And they
> worshipped the dragon which gave power unto
> the beast: and they worshipped the beast, saying,
> Who is like unto the beast? who is able to make

war with him? [5]And there was given unto him a mouth speaking great things and blasphemies; and power was given unto him to continue forty and two months. [6]And he opened his mouth in blasphemy against God, to blaspheme his name, and his tabernacle, and them that dwell in heaven. [7]And it was given unto him to make war with the saints, and to overcome them: and power was given him over all kindreds, and tongues, and nations. [8]And all that dwell upon the earth shall worship him, whose names are not written in the book of life of the Lamb slain from the foundation of the world. [9]If any man have an ear, let him hear. [10]He that leadeth into captivity shall go into captivity: he that killeth with the sword must be killed with the sword. Here is the patience and the faith of the saints. [11]And I beheld another beast coming up out of the earth; and he had two horns like a lamb, and he spake as a dragon. [12]And he exerciseth all the power of the first beast before him, and causeth the earth and them which dwell therein to worship the first beast, whose deadly wound was healed. [13]And he doeth great wonders, so that he maketh fire come down from heaven on the earth in the sight of men, [14]And deceiveth them that dwell on the earth by the means of those miracles which he had power to do in the sight of the beast; saying to them that dwell on the earth, that they should make an image to the beast, which had the wound by a sword, and did live. [15]And he had power to give life unto the image of the beast, that the image of the beast should both speak, and cause that as many as would not worship the image of the beast should be killed. [16]And he causeth all, both small and great, rich and poor, free and bond, to receive a mark in their right hand, or in their foreheads: [17]And that no man might buy or sell, save he that had the mark, or the name of the beast, or the number of his name. [18]Here is wisdom. Let him that hath understanding count the number of the beast: for it is the number of a man; and his number is Six hundred threescore and six. (Revelation 13:2–18)

Jesus speaks to us about this time in history and refers to the prophecy of Daniel. Please note that again, Jesus first talks about the Great Tribulation Period, and then he continues on from verse 31 to 51 of Matthew 24 in explaining the rapture of the believers which happens before the Tribulation Period. Please do not let this way of telling the story confuse you.

The very elect are the people who have received God's message during the Tribulation Period and now must keep the faith through powerful deception and, ultimately, death.

When ye therefore shall see the abomination of desolation, spoken of by Daniel the prophet, stand in the holy place, (whoso readeth, let him understand:) [16]Then let them which be in Judaea flee into the mountains: [17]Let him which is on the housetop not come down to take anything out of his house: [18]Neither let him which is in the field return back to take his clothes. [19]And woe unto them that are with child, and to them that give suck in those days! [20]But pray ye that your flight be not in the winter, neither on the sabbath day: [21]For then shall be great tribulation, such as was not since the beginning of the world to this time, no, nor ever shall be. [22]And except those days should be shortened, there should no flesh be saved: but for the elect's sake those days shall be shortened. [23]Then if any man shall say unto you, Lo, here is Christ, or there; believe it not. [24]For there shall arise false Christs, and false prophets, and shall shew great signs and wonders; insomuch that, if it were possible, they shall deceive the very elect. [25]Behold, I have told you before. [26]Wherefore if they shall say unto you, Behold, he is in the desert; go not forth: behold, he is in the secret chambers; believe it not. [27]For as the lightning cometh out of the east, and shineth even unto the west; so shall also the coming of the Son of man be. [28]For wheresoever the carcase is, there will the eagles be gathered together. [29]Immediately after the tribulation of those days shall the sun be darkened, and the moon shall not give her light, and the stars shall fall from heaven, and the powers of the heavens shall be shaken: [30]And then shall appear the sign of the Son of man in heaven: and then shall all the tribes of the earth mourn, and they shall see the Son of man coming in the clouds of heaven with power and great glory. (Matthew 24:15-30)

1) Why do the people remaining on earth believe the anti-christ is god? Who gives the anti-christ this power?
2) Why does the devil give power to do something that appears to be good?
3) Who did the anti-christ persecute, why, and how were they killed?
4) Who are the "very elect"? Why will it be so difficult to keep the faith in the tribulation period?

Memory Verse: 1 Corinthians 10:13

The devil
Created
Religion
to fool
Mankind

Calligraphy Designed By
Maria Grahl
www.wwapbglobal.com
@writewithapurpose

CHAPTER 9
THE FATE OF RELIGION

On Earth
Month 75–76

Remember that the religions of the world have made a compact with the worldwide religion in the name of peace. God has planted in each human the need to fellowship with Him. Now we know that the only way to fellowship with our Creator God is to have our sins cleansed as if we *never* sinned. This is why trusting in the innocent shed blood of Jesus as payment for our sins is the only way to justify ourselves and make ourselves worthy to fellowship with our Creator God, filling the void within each of us.

Throughout the ages, man has tried to fill the God-given void with many different pleasures that never fill the "God" void within each person. Since pleasures cannot fill the void, the devil created "religion" to fool mankind into thinking they can be good enough to fill the void in our lives. Religion has been very successful stealing money, time, and ruining lives with rituals that do nothing to please our Creator God.

The great whore represents the world's religions, and she gives her power and allegiance over to the political antichrist. The ten horns in this scripture are ten kings, and the seven heads are seven mountains on which the whore sits. This is part of Daniel's vision as well as John's vision.

And of the ten horns that were in his head, and of the other which came up, and before whom three fell; even of that horn that had eyes, and a mouth that spake very great things, whose look was more stout than his fellows. (Daniel 7:20)

The beast that thou sawest was, and is not; and shall ascend out of the bottomless pit, and go into perdition: and they that dwell on the earth shall wonder, whose names were not written in the book of life from the foundation of the world, when they behold the beast that was, and is not, and yet is. ⁹And here is the mind which hath wisdom. The seven heads are seven mountains, on which the woman sitteth. ¹⁰And there are seven kings: five are fallen, and one is, and the other is not yet come; and when he cometh, he must continue a short space. ¹¹And the beast that was, and is not, even he is the eighth, and is of the seven, and goeth into perdition. ¹²And the ten horns which thou sawest are ten kings, which have received no kingdom as yet; but receive power as kings one hour with the beast. ¹³These have one mind, and shall give their power and strength unto the beast. (Revelation 17:8–13)

The effect that the city of Babylon, (city on seven mountains) I believe to be recognized as a metaphor representing the world's religions, had on the rest of the world is explained in these verses. The devil uses the deception of religion in so many forms to draw man away from the Good News of the Gospel of Jesus Christ. Man tries to please their gods by their works, or they do not believe in a god at all because of the deception caused by religion.

The simple truth of God's grace was kept from them by crafty counterfeits for thousands of years sending the majority of mankind to an eternity apart from their loving Creator God.

These following verses also proclaim how wealth and human-ism were used by satan as well to draw mankind away from the saving Gospel of Jesus Christ.

And after these things I saw another angel come down from heaven, having great power; and the earth was lightened with his glory. ²And he cried mightily with a strong voice, saying, Babylon the great is fallen, is fallen, and is become the habitation of devils, and the hold of every foul spirit, and a cage of every unclean and hateful bird. ³For all nations have drunk of the wine of the wrath of her fornication, and the kings of the earth have committed fornication with her, and the merchants of the earth are waxed rich through the abundance of her delicacies. ⁴And I heard another voice from heaven, saying, Come out of her, my people, that ye be not partakers of her sins, and that ye receive not of her plagues. ⁵For her sins have reached unto heaven, and God hath remembered her iniquities. ⁶Reward her even as she rewarded you, and double unto her double according to her works: in the cup which she hath filled fill to her double. ⁷How much she hath glorified herself, and lived deliciously, so much torment and sorrow give her: for she saith in her heart, I sit a queen, and am no widow, and shall see no sorrow. ⁸Therefore shall her plagues come in one day, death, and mourning, and famine; and she shall be utterly burned with fire: for strong is the Lord God who judgeth her. ⁹And the kings of the earth, who have committed fornication and lived deliciously with her, shall bewail her, and lament for her, when they shall see the smoke of her burning, ¹⁰Standing afar off for the fear of her torment, saying, Alas, alas, that great city Babylon, that mighty city! for in one hour is thy judgment come. [11]And the merchants of the earth shall weep and mourn over her; for no man buyeth their merchandise any more: [12]The merchandise of gold, and silver, and precious stones, and of pearls, and fine linen, and purple, and silk, and scarlet, and all thyine wood, and all manner vessels of ivory, and all manner vessels of most precious wood, and of brass, and iron, and marble, [13]And cinnamon, and odours, and ointments, and frankincense, and wine, and oil, and fine flour, and wheat, and beasts, and sheep, and horses, and chariots, and slaves, and souls of men. [14]And the fruits that thy soul lusted after are departed from thee, and all things which were dainty and goodly are departed from thee, and thou shalt find them no more at all. [15]The merchants of these things, which were made rich by her, shall stand afar off for the fear of her torment, weeping and wailing, [16]And saying, Alas, alas, that great city, that was clothed in fine linen, and purple, and scarlet, and decked with gold, and precious stones, and pearls! [17]For in one hour so great riches is come to nought. And every shipmaster, and all the company in ships, and sailors, and as many as trade by sea, stood afar off, [18]And cried when they saw the smoke of her burning, saying, What city is like unto this great city! [19]And they cast dust on their heads, and cried, weeping and wailing, saying, Alas, alas, that great city, wherein were made rich all that had ships in the sea by reason of her costliness! for in one hour is she made desolate. [20]Rejoice over her, thou heaven, and ye holy apostles and prophets; for God hath avenged you on her. [21]And a mighty angel took up a stone like a great millstone, and cast it into the sea, saying, Thus with violence shall that great city Babylon be thrown down, and shall be found no more at all. [22]And the voice of harpers, and musicians, and of pipers, and trumpeters, shall be heard no more at all in thee; and no craftsman, of whatsoever craft he be, shall be found any more in thee; and the sound of a millstone shall be heard no more at all in thee; [23]And the light of a candle shall shine no more at all in thee; and the voice of the bridegroom and of the bride shall be heard no more at all in thee: for thy merchants were the great men of the earth; for by thy sorceries were all nations deceived. [24]And in her was found the blood of prophets, and of saints, and of all that were slain upon the earth. (Revelation 18:1–24)

In Heaven and On Earth
Month 75–76

About the seventy-fifth month, John sees the Raptured Saints in Heaven and the Tribulation Saints who were beheaded around the throne rejoicing as they see satan thrown to earth and the great whore (world's religions) destroyed.

The world turns its back on religion once and for all because they now know that they have been deceived by her and had their riches stolen by her. The ten kings of the earth are driven by God to destroy the religions of the world and give their power and allegiance over to the political antichrist.

And I saw another sign in heaven, great and marvellous, seven angels having the seven last plagues; for in them is filled up the wrath of God. [2]And I saw as it were a sea of glass mingled with fire: and them that had gotten the victory over the beast, and over his image, and over his mark, and over the number of his name, stand on the sea of glass, having the harps of God. ³And they sing the song of Moses the servant of God, and the song of the Lamb, saying, Great and marvellous are thy works, Lord God Almighty; just and true are thy ways, thou King of saints. ⁴Who shall not fear thee, O Lord, and glorify thy name? for thou only art holy: for all nations shall come and worship before thee; for thy judgments are made manifest. ⁵And after that I looked, and, behold, the temple of the tabernacle of the testimony in heaven was opened: ⁶And the seven angels came out of the temple, having the seven plagues, clothed in pure and white linen, and having their breasts girded with golden girdles. ⁷And one of the four beasts gave unto the seven angels seven golden vials full of the wrath of God, who liveth for ever and ever. ⁸And the temple was filled with smoke from the glory of God, and from his power; and no man was able to enter into the temple, till the seven plagues of the seven angels were fulfilled. (Revelation 15:1–8)

These shall make war with the Lamb, and the Lamb shall overcome them: for he is Lord of lords, and King of kings: and they that are with him are called, and chosen, and faithful. ¹⁵And he saith unto me, The waters which thou sawest, where the whore sitteth, are peoples, and multitudes, and nations, and tongues. ¹⁶And the ten horns which thou sawest upon the beast, these shall hate the whore, and shall make her desolate and naked, and shall eat her flesh, and burn her with fire. ¹⁷For God hath put in their hearts to fulfil his will, and to agree, and give their kingdom unto the beast, until the words of God shall be fulfilled. ¹⁸And the woman which thou sawest

is that great city, which reigneth over the kings of
the earth. (Revelation 17:14–18)

And after these things I heard a great voice of much
people in heaven, saying, Alleluia; Salvation, and
glory, and honour, and power, unto the Lord our
God: [2]For true and righteous are his judgments:
for he hath judged the great whore, which did
corrupt the earth with her fornication, and hath
avenged the blood of his servants at her hand.
[3]And again they said, Alleluia. And her smoke
rose up for ever and ever. [4]And the four and
twenty elders and the four beasts fell down and
worshipped God that sat on the throne, saying,
Amen; Alleluia. [5]And a voice came out of the
throne, saying, Praise our God, all ye his servants,
and ye that fear him, both small and great. [6]And I
heard as it were the voice of a great multitude, and
as the voice of many waters, and as the voice of
mighty thunderings, saying, Alleluia: for the Lord
God omnipotent reigneth. (Revelation 19:1–6)

1) What must we do that allows us to fellowship with our Creator God?
2) What is the devil's purpose to create religion? What is religion's effect on mankind
throughout the ages?
3) Describe how wealth and humanism are
used by satan to keep man from God's good
news. About the 75th month what happens
to satan?
4) When does the "judgement seat of Christ"
occur? What is happening in heaven during
the tribulation period?

Memory Verse: Proverbs 3:5,6

Scripture
Proclaims
that
God
Is Love

Calligraphy Designed By
Maria Grahl
www.wwapbglobal.com
@writewithapurpose

CHAPTER 10

GOD'S GRACE IN THE MIDST OF HIS JUSTICE

In Heaven and On Earth
Month 75–76

The scriptures proclaim that God is love and God shows His love in that He is still drawing His creation to himself even in the midst of His justice. God sends two prophets to earth around month thirty-four of the seventieth week for forty-two months to draw all remaining mankind to Him and to persuade them not to take the "mark" of the antichrist.

> And we have known and believed the love that
> God hath to us. God is love; and he that dwel-
> leth in love dwelleth in God, and God in him.
> (1 John 4:16)

Many are persuaded not to take the "mark" and paid with their lives. The fifth seal talks about the Tribulation Saints in a spiritual sense as they are "under the altar." The Tribulation Saints are treated, as were the people of the Old Testament covenant.

The Tribulation Saints will not have the Holy Spirit living within them like we are privileged today. They will be like the disciples when Jesus walked the earth with them. God spoke only through certain prophets just like in the Old Testament. They will not have the power of the Holy Spirit that we can draw upon today.

Some of the people who did not receive the "mark" will have been killed but more will be killed. The martyrs were given forgiveness symbolized by the giving of the "white robes." Remember, their sins are not paid by their deaths but by their faith in the innocent shed "blood of the Lamb."

> And when he had opened the fifth seal, I saw under the altar the souls of them that were slain for the word of God, and for the testimony which they held: [10]And they cried with a loud voice, saying, How long, O Lord, holy and true, dost thou not judge and avenge our blood on them that dwell on the earth? [11]And white robes were given unto every one of them; and it was said unto them, that they should rest yet for a little season, until their fellowservants also and their brethren, that should be killed as they were, should be fulfilled. (Revelation 6:9–11)

Around the seventy-sixth month, God's two witnesses (thought to be Enoch and Elijah) are killed, resurrected, and ascended into heaven. Please note that the same term is used, "come up hither," as in 4:1, announcing the Rapture of the Church. This is the same time the demons are released from the bottomless pit.

The beastly evil spirit that comes out of the bottomless pit enters into the political antichrist and is the person who kills the two prophets. After three and a half days, the prophets come back to life and ascend into heaven right in front of live television for all to see. This happens right in Jerusalem.

> And when they shall have finished their testimony, the beast that ascendeth out of the bottomless pit shall make war against them, and shall overcome them, and kill them. [8]And their dead bodies shall lie in the street of the great city, which spiritually is called Sodom and Egypt,

where also our Lord was crucified. ⁹And they of the people and kindreds and tongues and nations shall see their dead bodies three days and an half, and shall not suffer their dead bodies to be put in graves. ¹⁰And they that dwell upon the earth shall rejoice over them, and make merry, and shall send gifts one to another; because these two prophets tormented them that dwelt on the earth. ¹¹And after three days and an half the Spirit of life from God entered into them, and they stood upon their feet; and great fear fell upon them which saw them. ¹²And they heard a great voice from heaven saying unto them, Come up hither. And they ascended up to heaven in a cloud; and their enemies beheld them. ¹³And the same hour was there a great earthquake, and the tenth part of the city fell, and in the earthquake were slain of men seven thousand: and the remnant were affrighted, and gave glory to the God of heaven. (Revelation 11:7–13)

Remember, the antichrist has set himself up as god and has desecrated the temple in Jerusalem.

1) How does God show his love during the great tribulation period?

2) What must the people of the tribulation period not do? How is this a symbol of where they have their faith?

3) What is the difference between the Tribulation Saints and the bride of Christ taken in the rapture before the tribulation period? How does that realization make you feel now?

4) Why are the Tribulation Saints awarded entrance into heaven?

Memory Verse: Ephesians 6:12

1) In what month of the tribulation period are God's two witnesses killed? Describe what happens to these two prophets.
2) What event happens at the same time of their death?
3) How does that event play into their deaths?
4) How does what happens to the two witnesses resemble the rapture of the church?

Memory Verse: Proverbs 3:12

The Final Chance for satan to Destroy God's Creation

Calligraphy Designed By
Maria Grahl
www.wwapbglobal.com
@ @writewithapurpose

CHAPTER 11
GREAT TRIBULATION

The antichrist, both political and religious, broke the peace and began to take away the freedom of worship from the Jewish people by desecrating their temple and taking over Jerusalem in the forty-third month of the seventieth week. Any person who did not receive the "mark" of the antichrist was being beheaded for their newfound faith in Jesus as proclaimed by the two witnesses and new believers.

In Heaven, near the end of the seventieth week, are two types of saints: saints who overcame by the blood of the Lamb and the word of their testimony (Raptured believers) and saints who loved not their lives unto death (Tribulation Saints). All the saints are proclaimed to be preparing for the marriage supper of the Lamb and their triumphant appearance on earth with Jesus, their bridegroom, Savior, King of Kings, Lord of Lords, Creator God!

> And they overcame him by the blood of the Lamb, and by the word of their testimony; and they loved not their lives unto the death. (Revelation 12:11)

On Earth
Month 76–84

The sixth seal talks about the final unleashing from a heavenly perspective. Here we see the sun, moon, and stars affected. From an overhead perspective, we see the land affected (mountains and islands being removed—possible nuclear blasts causing enormous movement) with supernatural occurrences on earth including earthquakes, strong winds, etc. This time will correspond with the earthquake in Revelation 11:13 that took down a tenth part of Jerusalem at the time of the killing of the two witnesses.

Remember that only Jesus could begin the Tribulation Period. In verse 16 of chapter 6, John proclaims that this is the justice of the Lamb. This is a fuller explanation of the beginning of the Great Tribulation.

Please note that the timing of the Great Tribulation also corresponds with satan's final exit from God's presence. This is the final time for satan on earth to destroy God's creation.

> And I beheld when he had opened the sixth seal, and, lo, there was a great earthquake; and the sun became black as sackcloth of hair, and the moon became as blood; [13]And the stars of heaven fell unto the earth, even as a fig tree casteth her untimely figs, when she is shaken of a mighty wind. [14]And the heaven departed as a scroll when it is rolled together; and every mountain and island were moved out of their places. [15]And the kings of the earth, and the great men, and the rich men, and the chief captains, and the mighty men, and every bondman, and every free man, hid themselves in the dens and in the rocks of the mountains; [16]And said to the mountains and rocks, Fall on us, and hide us from the face of him that sitteth on the throne, and from the wrath of the Lamb: [17]For the great day of his wrath is come; and who shall be able to stand? (Revelation 6:12–17)

In Heaven
Month 76

Throughout the beginning of the seventieth week, Michael and his angels fight with the devil and his demons in the heavens. The devil has been accusing the believers before the throne of God since the beginning of time. The devil is defeated around the seventy-sixth month of the seventieth week and is cast out of Heaven for good. All the saints rejoiced!

> And there was war in heaven: Michael and his angels fought against the dragon; and the dragon fought and his angels, [8]And prevailed not; neither was their place found any more in heaven. [9]And the great dragon was cast out, that old serpent, called the devil, and satan, which deceiveth the whole world: he was cast out into the earth, and his angels were cast out with him. [10]And I heard a loud voice saying in heaven, Now is come salvation, and strength, and the kingdom of our God, and the power of his Christ: for the accuser of our brethren is cast down, which accused them before our God day and night. (Revelation 12:7–10)

On Earth
Month 76

About month seventy-six, the justice of God begins with the appearance of the Pale Horse of Death and the Fourth Seal. The first trumpet of judgement and the first vial is unleashed. Hail and fire mingled with blood hit the earth.

To a first century person seeing this vision, he might very well be trying to explain bombs of all kinds raining on mankind. It is written that a third of the earth is burned, and great pain is inflicted on the people with the "mark." It seems that God shields the people left who have not taken the "mark."

> And when he had opened the fourth seal, I heard the voice of the fourth beast say, Come and see. [8]And I looked, and behold a pale horse: and his name that sat on him was Death, and Hell followed with him. And power was given unto them

over the fourth part of the earth, to kill with sword, and with hunger, and with death, and with the beasts of the earth. (Revelation 6:7–8)

The first angel sounded, and there followed hail and fire mingled with blood, and they were cast upon the earth: and the third part of trees was burnt up, and all green grass was burnt up. (Revelation 8:7)

And I heard a great voice out of the temple saying to the seven angels, Go your ways, and pour out the vials of the wrath of God upon the earth. ²And the first went, and poured out his vial upon the earth; and there fell a noisome and grievous sore upon the men which had the mark of the beast, and upon them which worshipped his image. (Revelation 16:1–2)

On Earth
Month 76–77

The second trumpet and second vial affect the waters of the sea. Some kind of chemical warfare of massive bombing kills a third of the ocean's creatures. Possibly the sea in the passage is referring to the Mediterranean Sea. It is rumored that possibly the *chemical weapons of mass destruction* from Iraq are now in the sands of Syria (bordering the Mediterranean Sea) for this moment.

And the second angel sounded, and as it were a great mountain burning with fire was cast into the sea: and the third part of the sea became blood; ⁹And the third part of the creatures which were in the sea, and had life, died; and the third part of the ships were destroyed. (Revelation 8:8–9)

And the second angel poured out his vial upon the sea; and it became as the blood of a dead man: and every living soul died in the sea. (Revelation 16:3)

On Earth
Month 77

The third trumpet and third vial show a great star falling from heaven like a torch. This could mean large nuclear explosions that contaminate the waters of the earth. Many died from the poisoned waters. John may have been seeing visions of nuclear fallout and possibly chemical weapons poisoning the rivers and fountains of the earth.

And the third angel sounded, and there fell a great star from heaven, burning as it were a lamp, and it fell upon the third part of the rivers, and upon the fountains of waters; [11]And the name of the star is called Wormwood: and the third part of the waters became wormwood; and many men died of the waters, because they were made bitter. (Revelation 8:10–11)

And the third angel poured out his vial upon the rivers and fountains of waters; and they became blood. [5]And I heard the angel of the waters say, Thou art righteous, O Lord, which art, and wast, and shalt be, because thou hast judged thus. [6]For they have shed the blood of saints and prophets, and thou hast given them blood to drink; for they are worthy. [7]And I heard another out of the altar say, Even so, Lord God Almighty, true and righteous are thy judgments. (Revelation 16:4–7)

On Earth
Month 78

The fourth trumpet and vial are poured out on the earth. The fourth trumpet affects the sun, moon, and stars. Again, nuclear warfare creates huge clouds and could affect weather conditions, etc. John sees the sun causing a great heat, scorching men with fire. John could be trying to explain the site of nuclear-type blasts from the skies burning men like a mighty sun.

> And the fourth angel sounded, and the third part of the sun was smitten, and the third part of the moon, and the third part of the stars; so as the third part of them was darkened, and the day shone not for a third part of it, and the night likewise. [13]And I beheld, and heard an angel flying through the midst of heaven, saying with a loud voice, Woe, woe, woe, to the inhabiters of the earth by reason of the other voices of the trumpet of the three angels, which are yet to sound! (Revelation 8:12–13)

> And the fourth angel poured out his vial upon the sun; and power was given unto him to scorch men with fire. [9]And men were scorched with great heat, and blasphemed the name of God, which hath power over these plagues: and they repented not to give him glory. (Revelation 16:8–9)

On Earth
Month 79–84

About the seventy-ninth month on earth, the fifth trumpet and vial unleash the fury of the devil as the bottomless pit is opened. The devil knows that his time is very short to torment God's creation. It is written that this torment lasts five months.

John possibly saw helicopters shooting missiles and all kinds of weapons. This could also mean a spiritual torment as satan and his demons are allowed all-out torture of man except he is not allowed to kill. Man will cry out to be killed to no avail. In verse 4, the men not with the seal of God will be tormented. The men with the seal of God are those who have not taken the "mark" of the beast and have not been martyred yet.

> And the fifth angel sounded, and I saw a star fall from heaven unto the earth: and to him was given the key of the bottomless pit. [2]And he opened the bottomless pit; and there arose a smoke out of the pit, as the smoke of a great furnace; and the sun and the air were darkened by reason of the smoke of the pit. [3]And there came out of the smoke locusts upon the earth: and unto them was given power, as the scorpions of the earth have power. [4]And it was commanded them that they should not hurt the grass of the earth, neither any green thing, neither any tree; but only those men which have not the seal of God in their foreheads. [5]And to them it was given that they should not kill them, but that they should be tormented five months: and their torment was as the torment of a scorpion, when he striketh a man. [6]And in those days shall men seek death, and shall not find it; and shall desire to die, and death shall flee from them. [7]And the shapes of the locusts were like unto horses prepared unto battle; and on their heads were as it were crowns like gold, and their faces were as the faces of men. [8]And they had hair as the hair of women, and their teeth were as the teeth of lions. [9]And they had breastplates, as it were breastplates of iron; and the sound of their wings was as the sound of chariots of many horses running to battle. [10]And

they had tails like unto scorpions, and there were
stings in their tails: and their power was to hurt
men five months. ¹¹And they had a king over
them, which is the angel of the bottomless pit,
whose name in the Hebrew tongue is Abaddon,
but in the Greek tongue hath his name Apollyon.
¹²One woe is past; and, behold, there come two
woes more hereafter. (Revelation 9:1–12)

The kingdom is in darkness possibly from the smoke from the
warfare. The people cursed God because of their pains and sores and
did not repent of their evil. This is when the devil focuses his full
wrath on the peoples of the earth. The devil torments everyone but
truly hates the Jewish people because they brought our Savior into
the world. The devil will set out to find all Jewish people and any
person who has not taken the "mark."

The Jewish people have been in hiding for three and a half years
since the temple was desecrated by the antichrist. The Jewish people
are protected by God so that satan is not able to harm them. The
only people satan could harm were the people who had the "mark"
of the antichrist.

Therefore rejoice, ye heavens, and ye that dwell
in them. Woe to the inhabiters of the earth and
of the sea! for the devil is come down unto you,
having great wrath, because he knoweth that he
hath but a short time. ¹³And when the dragon
saw that he was cast unto the earth, he persecuted
the woman which brought forth the man child.
¹⁴And to the woman were given two wings of a
great eagle, that she might fly into the wilderness, into her place, where she is nourished for
a time, and times, and half a time, from the face
of the serpent. ¹⁵And the serpent cast out of his
mouth water as a flood after the woman, that he
might cause her to be carried away of the flood.

[16]And the earth helped the woman, and the earth opened her mouth, and swallowed up the flood which the dragon cast out of his mouth. [17]And the dragon was wroth with the woman, and went to make war with the remnant of her seed, which keep the commandments of God, and have the testimony of Jesus Christ. (Revelation 12:12–17)

And there followed another angel, saying, Babylon is fallen, is fallen, that great city, because she made all nations drink of the wine of the wrath of her fornication. [9]And the third angel followed them, saying with a loud voice, If any man worship the beast and his image, and receive his mark in his forehead, or in his hand, [10]The same shall drink of the wine of the wrath of God, which is poured out without mixture into the cup of his indignation; and he shall be tormented with fire and brimstone in the presence of the holy angels, and in the presence of the Lamb: [11]And the smoke of their torment ascendeth up for ever and ever: and they have no rest day nor night, who worship the beast and his image, and whosoever receiveth the mark of his name. (Revelation 14:8–11)

And the fifth angel poured out his vial upon the seat of the beast; and his kingdom was full of darkness; and they gnawed their tongues for pain, [11]And blasphemed the God of heaven because of their pains and their sores, and repented not of their deeds. (Revelation 16:10–11)

On Earth
Month 80–84

The sixth trumpet and vial bring the armies of the east on the scene. They have an army of two hundred thousand thousand or 200,000,000 (200 million) soldiers. This many soldiers exist in the east today! They cross the River Euphrates, possibly like our armies crossed the river on large barges, as if on dry land. Again, this type of equipment has never been seen by a first-century man, causing him to proclaim that the river has dried up.

The king from the east and the "bear" of the north begin to ascend on the Middle East about the time the antichrist desecrates the temple in Jerusalem in the forty-third month. Please understand that the reason for their coming may not be understood or may be for many different reasons.

They will come with weapons killing many, even a third of mankind. This is a supernatural battle. The dragon and false prophet send out demons to draw all men of the earth to battle. The people of the earth were drawn to a place called Armageddon, to a valley called Megiddo.

I also believe the entire world will take part in the worship of the antichrist, the rejection of religion, and the killing of the Tribulation Saints. Every corner of the earth will be affected by the plagues and death. The Middle East will be the focal point of the final battle and culmination of the end of time as we now know.

> And the sixth angel sounded, and I heard a voice from the four horns of the golden altar which is before God, [14]Saying to the sixth angel which had the trumpet, Loose the four angels which are bound in the great river Euphrates. [15]And the four angels were loosed, which were prepared for an hour, and a day, and a month, and a year, for to slay the third part of men. [16]And the number of the army of the horsemen were two hundred thousand thousand: and I heard the number of

them. ¹⁷And thus I saw the horses in the vision, and them that sat on them, having breastplates of fire, and of jacinth, and brimstone: and the heads of the horses were as the heads of lions; and out of their mouths issued fire and smoke and brimstone. ¹⁸By these three was the third part of men killed, by the fire, and by the smoke, and by the brimstone, which issued out of their mouths. ¹⁹For their power is in their mouth, and in their tails: for their tails were like unto serpents, and had heads, and with them they do hurt. ²⁰And the rest of the men which were not killed by these plagues yet repented not of the works of their hands, that they should not worship devils, and idols of gold, and silver, and brass, and stone, and of wood: which neither can see, nor hear, nor walk: ²¹Neither repented they of their murders, nor of their sorceries, nor of their fornication, nor of their thefts. (Revelation 9:13–21)

And the sixth angel poured out his vial upon the great river Euphrates; and the water thereof was dried up, that the way of the kings of the east might be prepared. ¹³And I saw three unclean spirits like frogs come out of the mouth of the dragon, and out of the mouth of the beast, and out of the mouth of the false prophet. ¹⁴For they are the spirits of devils, working miracles, which go forth unto the kings of the earth and of the whole world, to gather them to the battle of that great day of God Almighty. ¹⁶And he gathered them together into a place called in the Hebrew tongue Armageddon. (Revelation 16:12–14,16)

1) Who are the two types of saints in heaven during the tribulation period? For what are they preparing?
2) What corresponds with the timing of the Great Tribulation? Why is this significant?
3) What is happening around month 76 in heaven? How does this event affect the saints?

Memory Verse: Romans 3:10

1) What horse, seal, trumpet, and vial represent what begins to happen in the 76th month on earth? Describe what happens during this first event.
2) What does the second trumpet and vial bring upon the earth?
3) What did John see during the third trumpet and vial? What current event is a first century person trying to explain?
4) What is John possibly trying to explain during the vision of the fourth trumpet and vial?
5) What does the fifth trumpet and vial bring upon the earth? Why does man wish to die and cannot die?
6) How large is the army of the sixth trumpet and vial? Why do these armies come to the Armageddon?

Memory Verse: John 5:24

The coming
of the
Lord with
His
Bride

Calligraphy Designed By
Maria Grahl
www.wwapbglobal.com
@ @writewithapurpose

CHAPTER 12

GREAT AND TERRIBLE DAY OF THE LORD

In Heaven
Month 77–84

In Jewish marriage tradition, the celebration continues for seven days! The consummation of the marriage, in my opinion, is the "judgment seat" of Christ. I believe the "judgement seat" of Christ occurs immediately after the rapture of the bride.

The celebration of the marriage between the Lamb, Jesus Christ, our bridegroom, occurs during the entire "week of years," culminating with the marriage supper of the Lamb just before all leave Heaven to rule and reign with Jesus for a thousand years on earth.

> Let us be glad and rejoice, and give honour to him: for the marriage of the Lamb is come, and his wife hath made herself ready. ⁸And to her was granted that she should be arrayed in fine linen, clean and white: for the fine linen is the righteousness of saints. ⁹And he saith unto me, Write, Blessed are they which are called unto the marriage supper of the Lamb. And he saith unto me, These are the true sayings of God. ¹⁰And I fell at his feet to worship him. And he said unto me, See thou do it not: I am thy fellowservant, and of thy brethren that have the testimony of Jesus:

worship God: for the testimony of Jesus is the spirit of prophecy. (Revelation 19:7-10)

On Earth and In Heaven
Month 84

The seventh trumpet sounds along with the pouring of the seventh vial proclaiming the coming of the Lord with His bride, the Raptured Saints and the Tribulation Saints, to end the "battle of Armageddon" and begin the 1,000-year reign of Jesus and His bride on earth. This signals the end of the seventieth week of Daniel's vision.

A massive earthquake occurs as Jesus sets foot on the Mount of Olives, splitting it in two.

> And his feet shall stand in that day upon the mount of Olives, which is before Jerusalem on the east, and the mount of Olives shall cleave in the midst thereof toward the east and toward the west, and there shall be a very great valley; and half of the mountain shall remove toward the north, and half of it toward the south. (Zechariah 14:4)

Large hail falls from Heaven. It may have looked like large hail falling from Heaven as the skies were filled with the saints coming in the clouds to end the war. The whole world will immediately fall to their knees in surrender by the sheer power of the Lamb of God.

> And I saw another mighty angel come down from heaven, clothed with a cloud: and a rainbow was upon his head, and his face was as it were the sun, and his feet as pillars of fire: [2]And he had in his hand a little book open: and he set his right foot upon the sea, and his left foot on the earth, [3]And cried with a loud voice, as when a lion roareth: and when he had cried, seven thun-

ders uttered their voices. ⁴And when the seven thunders had uttered their voices, I was about to write: and I heard a voice from heaven saying unto me, Seal up those things which the seven thunders uttered, and write them not. ⁵And the angel which I saw stand upon the sea and upon the earth lifted up his hand to heaven, ⁶And sware by him that liveth for ever and ever, who created heaven, and the things that therein are, and the earth, and the things that therein are, and the sea, and the things which are therein, that there should be time no longer: ⁷But in the days of the voice of the seventh angel, when he shall begin to sound, the mystery of God should be finished, as he hath declared to his servants the prophets. (Revelation 10:1–7)

The second woe is past; and, behold, the third woe cometh quickly. ¹⁵And the seventh angel sounded; and there were great voices in heaven, saying, The kingdoms of this world are become the kingdoms of our Lord, and of his Christ; and he shall reign for ever and ever. ¹⁶And the four and twenty elders, which sat before God on their seats, fell upon their faces, and worshipped God, ¹⁷Saying, We give thee thanks, O Lord God Almighty, which art, and wast, and art to come; because thou hast taken to thee thy great power, and hast reigned. ¹⁸And the nations were angry, and thy wrath is come, and the time of the dead, that they should be judged, and that thou shouldest give reward unto thy servants the prophets, and to the saints, and them that fear thy name, small and great; and shouldest destroy them which destroy the earth. ¹⁹And the temple of God was opened in heaven, and there was seen in his temple the ark of his testament: and there were lightnings, and voices, and thunderings, and an earthquake, and great hail. (Revelation 11:14–19)

On earth
Month 84

God's justice is poured out on the earth for the evil that has been done to the saints of the Lord. The fact that the grapes are ripe means that the time is right for the justice of God. This justice is like the justice that was poured out on all mankind because of its evil during the flood when only Noah and his family were saved.

Here is the patience of the saints: here are they that keep the commandments of God, and the faith of Jesus. [13]And I heard a voice from heaven saying unto me, Write, Blessed are the dead which die in the Lord from henceforth: Yea, saith the Spirit, that they may rest from their labours; and their works do follow them. [14]And I looked, and behold a white cloud, and upon the cloud one sat like unto the Son of man, having on his head a golden crown, and in his hand a sharp sickle. [15]And another angel came out of the temple, crying with a loud voice to him that sat on the cloud, Thrust in thy sickle, and reap: for the time is come for thee to reap; for the harvest of the earth is ripe. [16]And he that sat on the cloud thrust in his sickle on the earth; and the earth was reaped. [17]And another angel came out of the temple which is in heaven, he also having a sharp sickle. [18]And another angel came out from the altar, which had power over fire; and cried with a loud cry to him that had the sharp sickle, saying, Thrust in thy sharp sickle, and gather the clusters of the vine of the earth; for her grapes are fully ripe. [19]And the angel thrust in his sickle into the earth, and gathered the vine of the earth, and cast it into the great winepress of the wrath of God. [20]And the winepress was trodden without the city, and blood came out of the winepress, even unto the horse bridles, by the space of a thousand and six hundred furlongs. (Revelation 14:12–20)

And the seventh angel poured out his vial into the air; and there came a great voice out of the temple of heaven, from the throne, saying, It is done. [18]And there were voices, and thunders, and lightnings; and there was a great earthquake, such as was not since men were upon the earth, so mighty an earthquake, and so great. [19]And the great city was divided into three parts, and the cities of the nations fell: and great Babylon came in remembrance before God, to give unto her the cup of the wine of the fierceness of his wrath. [20]And every island fled away, and the mountains were not found. [21]And there fell upon men a great hail out of heaven, every stone about the weight of a talent: and men blasphemed God because of the plague of the hail; for the plague thereof was exceeding great. (Revelation 16:17–21)

In Heaven and On Earth
Month 84

This is a beautiful picture of Jesus, our bridegroom, coming in triumph along with all of His saints to end Armageddon and set up His earthly reign for a thousand years. God directs the fowls of the earth to "clean up" the dead from the earth. I can assure you that it is not a pretty sight. Sin never is a pretty sight.

The political antichrist and the false prophet are immediately cast in the "lake of fire and brimstone" forever. These are the first to be cast in the "Lake of Fire," the place of final judgement that was ultimately prepared for satan and his demons.

> And I saw heaven opened, and behold a white horse; and he that sat upon him was called Faithful and True, and in righteousness he doth judge and make war. ¹²His eyes were as a flame of fire, and on his head were many crowns; and he had a name written, that no man knew, but he himself. ¹³And he was clothed with a vesture dipped in blood: and his name is called The Word of God. ¹⁴And the armies which were in heaven followed him upon white horses, clothed in fine linen, white and clean. ¹⁵And out of his mouth goeth a sharp sword, that with it he should smite the nations: and he shall rule them with a rod of iron: and he treadeth the winepress of the fierceness and wrath of Almighty God. ¹⁶And he hath on his vesture and on his thigh a name written, KING OF KINGS, AND LORD OF LORDS. ¹⁷And I saw an angel standing in the sun; and he cried with a loud voice, saying to all the fowls that fly in the midst of heaven, Come and gather yourselves together unto the supper of the great God; ¹⁸That ye may eat the flesh of kings, and the flesh of captains, and the flesh of mighty men, and the flesh of horses, and of them that sit on them, and the flesh of all men, both free and bond, both small and great. ¹⁹And I saw the beast, and the kings of the earth, and their armies, gathered together to make war against him that sat on the horse, and against his army. ²⁰And the beast was taken, and with him the false prophet that wrought miracles before him, with which he deceived them that had received the mark of the beast, and them that worshipped his

image. These both were cast alive into a lake of fire burning with brimstone. [21]And the remnants are then slain with the sword of him that sat upon the horse, which sword proceeded out of his mouth: and all the fowls were filled with their flesh. (Revelation 19:11–21)

1) What does the seventh trumpet and vial proclaim?
2) What marks the end of the great tribulation period?
3) What happens when Jesus sets His foot on the Mount of Olives?
4) What do the inhabitants of earth do when they see Jesus arriving with His saints?
5) Who is immediately cast into the "lake of fire"? What is God's purpose for the "lake of fire"?

Memory Verse: Romans 3:23

The devil
and
his demons
are
BOUND!

Calligraphy Designed By
Maria Grahl
www.wwapbglobal.com
@writewithapurpose

CHAPTER 13
PEACE ON EARTH

The 1,000-Year
Reign on Earth

The devil and his demons are bound and cast into the "bottomless" pit for 1,000 years. Verse 3 proclaims that the devil will be loosed for a little season after the 1,000 years.

This is indeed 1,000 years of peace and bliss as the saints dwell with our bridegroom, Jesus. We are free from trouble, temptations, and sadness. The deceiver satan is bound along with his demons and cannot touch any of God's creation. I would say this should be peace.

> And I saw an angel come down from heaven, having the key of the bottomless pit and a great chain in his hand. ²And he laid hold on the dragon, that old serpent, which is the Devil, and Satan, and bound him a thousand years, ³And cast him into the bottomless pit, and shut him up, and set a seal upon him, that he should deceive the nations no more, till the thousand years should be fulfilled: and after that he must be loosed a little season. (Revelation 20:1–3)

The Raptured Saints are found on thrones and were given judgement to rule over the earth. Also, the Tribulation Saints were there, and they are to live and reign with Christ for the 1,000 years.

The Raptured Saints are given judgement to rule on the earth for 1,000 years while satan is bound. The fact that we are given the power to judge implies that there will be reason to judge. Apparently, the people that are left and dwell on the earth will have the nature to sin and need to be directed or judged.

I am sure the Tribulation Saints will have a position in Heaven and earth as well during the 1,000 years. The very fact that they did not believe before the rapture puts them into a different position than the saints who believe without entering the Tribulation Period. Jesus is the perfect judge, and I leave all judgement in His hands regarding the differences if any.

My plea to you is to put your faith in what Jesus has done for you on this side of the rapture of the believers. Waiting to see what happens may very well be your doom. Even the very elect who know the truth but do not act on it will be deceived by the false prophet and antichrist. Do not wait!

> And I saw thrones, and they sat upon them, and judgment was given unto them: and I saw the souls of them that were beheaded for the witness of Jesus, and for the word of God, and which had not worshipped the beast, neither his image, neither had received his mark upon their foreheads, or in their hands; and they lived and reigned with Christ a thousand years. (Revelation 20:4)

The people who died during the Great Tribulation having the "mark" of the antichrist, along with the people who did not rapture, will not live again until after the 1,000-year reign of Jesus and His bride (Raptured Saints and Tribulation Saints). The scriptures say they will sleep in their graves waiting for the great Judgement Day.

> But the rest of the dead lived not again until the thousand years were finished. This is the first resurrection. (Revelation 20:5)

1) What happens to the devil and his demons?

2) Describe the 1,000 years for the saints?
3) What will the saints be doing during the 1,000 year reign on earth with Jesus?
4) What happens to all of the non-believers?

Memory Verse: John 1:12

Lake of fire created for satan and his demons

CHAPTER 14

GREAT WHITE THRONE OF JUDGEMENT

After the 1,000-Year
Reign on Earth

After the 1,000-year reign of Jesus on earth with His bride is finished, the devil is loosed from the bottomless pit for a short season. The devil gathers the people of the earth again to do battle with Jesus and the bride.

The people now number as the sands of the sea after 1,000 years. John sees the city of Jerusalem encircled with the people of the earth driven by the evil spirit of the devil for one last time. Verse 9 proclaims that God showers fire down from heaven devouring the armies of the devil in a moment ending the war.

> And when the thousand years are expired, Satan shall be loosed out of his prison, ⁸And shall go out to deceive the nations which are in the four quarters of the earth, Gog and Magog, to gather them together to battle: the number of whom is as the sand of the sea. ⁹And they went up on the breadth of the earth, and compassed the camp of the saints about, and the beloved city: and fire came down from God out of heaven, and devoured them. (Revelation 20:7–9)

The devil and his demons are cast into the "lake of fire and brimstone" with the beast (political antichrist) and false prophet (spiritual antichrist) to be tormented forever and ever, never to be loosed again. This is the Great White Throne of Judgement where all the dead are resurrected to stand before judgement. Verse 15 makes it plain that everyone who is not found in the Book of Life will be cast into the "lake of fire" to be tormented forever and ever.

The "small and great," I believe, refers to what they thought of themselves. The religious leaders thought they were above reproach and yet found themselves lost because their faith was in their works and not in what Jesus did for us on the cross of Calvary alone.

I also believe that the "books" that are opened are their memories. All is remembered, and nothing is really forgotten. Their own memories will condemn them of sin and send them to an eternity without God in the "lake of fire" created for satan and his demons.

> And the devil that deceived them was cast into the lake of fire and brimstone, where the beast and the false prophet are, and shall be tormented day and night for ever and ever. (Revelation 20:10)

> And I saw a great white throne, and him that sat on it, from whose face the earth and the heaven fled away; and there was found no place for them. ¹²And I saw the dead, small and great, stand before God; and the books were opened: and another book was opened, which is the book of life: and the dead were judged out of those things which were written in the books, according to their works. ¹³And the sea gave up the dead which were in it; and death and hell delivered up the dead which were in them: and they were judged every man according to their works. ¹⁴And death and hell were cast into the lake of fire. This is the second death. ¹⁵And whosoever was not found written in the book of life was cast into the lake of fire. (Revelation 20:11–15)

1) What happens to the devil and his demons after the 1,000 years is over?
2) What does God do to protect the saints against the army of satan?
3) What happens to satan and his demons?
4) Who is cast into the "lake of fire" at the great white throne of judgement?
5) What is possibly referred to as the "books" that are opened? How will these books affect mankind?
6) What is possibly referred to as the "small and great"?

Memory Verse: Romans 12:19

Raptured
Saints
are called
the
Bride of
Christ

Calligraphy Designed By
Maria Grahl
www.wwapbglobal.com
@writewithapurpose

Chapter 15
The Promise

The New Heaven
and New Earth

Jesus gives John a vision of the new Heaven and the new earth. This is a vision that the people of the twentieth century would not be able to fully comprehend. Scripture says that God will dwell there in the New Jerusalem along with all who are written in the Lamb's Book of Life.

The Raptured Saints are called the bride of Christ! After ruling and reigning with Jesus for a thousand years, it appears that we will be adorned as a glorious, holy city prepared for her bridegroom. Real life with our Creator God will begin forever and ever!

Verse seven talks about overcoming which means all who hold the faith in what Jesus did for all at the cross of Calvary. That is it! The innocent shed blood of Jesus Christ, our bridegroom, has paid for our perfection, our holiness. We can only worship Him with thankfulness and reverence.

> And I saw a new heaven and a new earth: for the first heaven and the first earth were passed away; and there was no more sea. ²And I John saw the holy city, new Jerusalem, coming down from God out of heaven, prepared as a bride adorned for her husband. ³And I heard a great voice out of heaven saying, Behold, the tabernacle of God

is with men, and he will dwell with them, and they shall be his people, and God himself shall be with them, and be their God. ⁴And God shall wipe away all tears from their eyes; and there shall be no more death, neither sorrow, nor crying, neither shall there be any more pain: for the former things are passed away. ⁵And he that sat upon the throne said, Behold, I make all things new. And he said unto me, Write: for these words are true and faithful. ⁶And he said unto me, It is done. I am Alpha and Omega, the beginning and the end. I will give unto him that is athirst of the fountain of the water of life freely. ⁷He that overcometh shall inherit all things; and I will be his God, and he shall be my son. ⁸But the fearful, and unbelieving, and the abominable, and murderers, and whoremongers, and sorcerers, and idolaters, and all liars, shall have their part in the lake which burneth with fire and brimstone: which is the second death. (Revelation 21:1–8)

The following verses confirm that the holy city, New Jerusalem, is in fact the glorious city where the bride of Christ will dwell for eternity! God is so precise on what He has for us that He gives John a vision of the exact dimensions and exact construction details!

Are you written in the Lamb's Book of Life? You can know beyond any shadow of doubt! Refer back to chapter 1 and make a decision to put your F-A-I-T-H in what Jesus has already accomplished for you.

And there came unto me one of the seven angels which had the seven vials full of the seven last plagues, and talked with me, saying, Come hither, I will shew thee the bride, the Lamb's wife. ¹⁰And he carried me away in the spirit to a great and high mountain, and shewed me that great city, the holy Jerusalem, descending out of heaven from God, [11]Having the glory of God: and her light was like unto a stone most precious, even like a jasper stone, clear as crystal; [12]And had a wall great and high, and had twelve gates, and at the gates twelve angels, and names written thereon, which are the names of the twelve tribes of the children of Israel: [13]On the east three gates; on the north three gates; on the south three gates; and on the west three gates. [14]And the wall of the city had twelve foundations, and in them the names of the twelve apostles of the Lamb. [15]And he that talked with me had a golden reed to measure the city, and the gates thereof, and the wall thereof. [16]And the city lieth foursquare, and the length is as large as the breadth: and he measured the city with the reed, twelve thousand furlongs. The length and the breadth and the height of it are equal. [17]And he measured the wall thereof, an hundred and forty and four cubits, according to the measure of a man, that is, of the angel. [18]And the building of the wall of it was of jasper: and the city was pure gold, like unto clear glass. [19]And the foundations of the wall of the city were garnished with all manner of precious stones. The first foundation was jasper; the second, sapphire; the third, a chalcedony; the fourth, an emerald; [20]The fifth, sardonyx; the sixth, sardius; the seventh, chrysolite; the eighth, beryl; the ninth, a topaz; the tenth, a chrysoprasus; the eleventh, a jacinth; the twelfth, an amethyst. [21]And the twelve gates were twelve pearls; every several gate was of one pearl: and the street of the city was pure gold, as it were transparent glass. [22]And I saw no temple therein: for the Lord God Almighty and the Lamb are the temple of it. [23]And the city had

no need of the sun, neither of the moon, to shine
in it: for the glory of God did lighten it, and the
Lamb is the light thereof. [24]And the nations of
them which are saved shall walk in the light of
it: and the kings of the earth do bring their glory
and honour into it. [25]And the gates of it shall not
be shut at all by day: for there shall be no night
there. [26]And they shall bring the glory and honour of the nations into it. [27]And there shall in no
wise enter into it any thing that defileth, neither
whatsoever worketh abomination, or maketh
a lie: but they which are written in the Lamb's
book of life. (Revelation 21:9–27)

John describes as best he can the "river of life" that will flow
from the throne of God and the "perfect light" that will continually
shine from the light of the Lamb (Jesus). There will be no night
there, and darkness will be no more. The bride will dwell with the
bridegroom forever and ever.

Remember that Adam and Eve were driven from the Garden
of Eden and the "tree of life" because if they ate of the "tree of life,"
knowing good and evil, they would have lived forever in their sin.
That is how dire the situation. In the new Heaven and new earth we
find the "tree of life!"

And he shewed me a pure river of water of life,
clear as crystal, proceeding out of the throne of
God and of the Lamb. [2]In the midst of the street
of it, and on either side of the river, was there the
tree of life, which bare twelve manner of fruits,
and yielded her fruit every month: and the leaves
of the tree were for the healing of the nations.
[3]And there shall be no more curse: but the throne
of God and of the Lamb shall be in it; and his servants shall serve him: [4]And they shall see his face;
and his name shall be in their foreheads. [5]And

there shall be no night there; and they need no candle, neither light of the sun; for the Lord God giveth them light: and they shall reign for ever and ever. (Revelation 22:1–5)

Right now!

The final verses of Revelation proclaim that we are not to keep these prophecies to ourselves. The Lord proclaims that these things will soon come to pass. Remember that 1,000 years with the Lord is as one day. This is a reminder that there is no time in the spirit realm.

Jesus, the Alpha and Omega, will reward all according to our works. If you have not chosen to rely on God's free gift of salvation, you will be judged by your works at the Great White Throne of Judgement.

If you have chosen to trust in Christ's shed blood as payment for your sins "alone," Jesus will reward you according to the works you have done *after* you put your F-A-I-T-H in what He did for you on the cross. Jesus will do this for you at His "judgement seat" in Heaven after He raptures you to Heaven.

Verse 11 tells us to share the Gospel of Christ, but do not force your beliefs on anyone. The decision to follow Christ and embrace the shed blood of Christ as their personal payment for their sin is completely a personal decision that only the person can decide.

No matter what happens, never give up the faith!

And he said unto me, These sayings are faithful and true: and the Lord God of the holy prophets sent his angel to shew unto his servants the things which must shortly be done. ⁷Behold, I come quickly: blessed is he that keepeth the sayings of the prophecy of this book. ⁸And I John saw these things, and heard them. And when I had heard and seen, I fell down to worship before the feet of the angel which shewed me these things. ⁹Then saith he unto me, See thou do it not: for

I am thy fellowservant, and of thy brethren the prophets, and of them which keep the sayings of this book: worship God. [10]And he saith unto me, Seal not the sayings of the prophecy of this book: for the time is at hand. [11]He that is unjust, let him be unjust still: and he which is filthy, let him be filthy still: and he that is righteous, let him be righteous still: and he that is holy, let him be holy still. [12]And, behold, I come quickly; and my reward is with me, to give every man according as his work shall be. [13]I am Alpha and Omega, the beginning and the end, the first and the last. (Revelation 22:6–13)

These words are for us today. Jesus says, "Drink of the 'water of life' freely." Embrace the Good News of God's Grace for you today for Jesus says, "surely I come quickly."

Yes, doing His commandments in His power will give you the highest blessing. When Jesus calls us to do his commandments, He knows that the *only* way you can enjoy eternity with Him is that you must go through Him. Remember, He called Himself the "door." Jesus is the "door" to heaven. His first commandment is to open your door to Him as in Revelation 3:20.

Behold, I stand at the door, and knock: if any man hear my voice, and open the door, I will come in to him, and will sup with him, and he with me. (Revelation 3:20)

Blessed are they that do his commandments that they may have right to the tree of life, and may enter in through the gates into the city. [15]For without are dogs, and sorcerers, and whoremongers, and murderers, and idolaters, and whosoever loveth and maketh a lie. [16]I Jesus have sent mine angel to testify unto you these things in the churches. I am the root and the offspring of David, and the bright and morning star. [17]And the Spirit and the bride say, Come. And let him that heareth say, Come. And let him that is athirst come. And whosoever will, let him take the water of life freely. [18]For I testify unto every man that heareth the words of the prophecy of this book, If any man shall add unto these things, God shall add unto him the plagues that are written in this book: [19]And if any man shall take away from the words of the book of this prophecy, God shall take away his part out of the book of life, and out of the holy city, and from the things which are written in this book. [20]He which testifieth these things saith, Surely I come quickly. Amen. Even so, come, Lord Jesus. [21]The grace of our Lord Jesus Christ be with you all. Amen. (Revelation 22:14–21)

1) What does God create for Himself and His bride?
2) What does the New Jerusalem look like to John? What does the angel confirm?
3) Describe the new heaven and new earth according to the vision.
4) Why is the "river of life" so important?

Memory Verse: Hebrews 11:6

1) What are those not found in the "Book of Life" judged by at the great white throne? What sends mankind to the "lake of fire"?
2) If you have put your faith in the shed blood of Jesus Christ, how will Jesus judge your

works? (Before salvation and after salvation) How is this judgment different than the Great White Throne Judgement?

3) What is the only way you can spend eternity with Jesus, your Creator God?

4) Share your testimony of when you placed your faith in the shed blood of Jesus Christ alone as payment for your sins. Please be truthful with yourself. Ask God to search your heart. If you cannot find a specific moment, make one right now!

5) Write out your personal goals for your life now that you know more about God's love for you, His purpose for you, and God's future for you.

Memory Verse: 1 John 4:4; Romans 8:37

About the Author

Nate Grahl, a graduate of Bible College and a John C. Maxwell Leadership Team member, has served on various mission trips and travels internationally as the CEO of a multimillion-dollar corporation. Nate has had an interest in the Book of Revelation since his early twenties.

Many experiences have shaped and solidified Nate's faith. In 2012, a drunk driver tragically took the life of Nate's father. This event challenged Nate's faith causing him to question, "Who is God?" Through searching the scriptures, Nate came to the conclusion that God is love, and we are not able to understand everything. Nate found peace and love in his decision.

This book is an extension of Nate's studies and lifelong experiences. Nate trusts that God is our guide into all truth. Nate explains that there are aspects of Revelation that are still a mystery, but as you will read, they are not a necessity to understanding God's plan.

Nate's study of Revelation has brought him hope for the future, and he desires each and every person to experience this same hope, inner peace, and love.